"Rohadi Nagassar has given the church a powerful gift. By sharing his own stories interlaced with stories from the community and Scripture, he invites us to reconsider belonging, liberation, and freedom together in ways that will lead to flourishing. As so many of us grapple with deconstruction, Nagassar has provided an embodied path of true belonging, not in spite of our questions, doubts, or discomforts with church, but because of them."

**SARAH BESSEY,** New York Times bestselling author of A Rhythm of Prayer and Jesus Feminist

"*When We Belong* captures Jesus' core message of belonging. The gospel communicates the simple but powerful truth that those marginalized, pushed aside, and overlooked are no longer outsiders—rather, they are people worthy of being included in God's beloved community. This book not only reminds us of this truth but seeks to refuel those who have lost hope and faith along the way. If you have been tired and weary on your faith journey and are looking for words to remind you that belonging is the way forward, then Rohadi Nagassar's book is for you."

**TERENCE LESTER,** founder of Love Beyond Walls and author of When We Stand: The Power of Seeking Justice Together and I See You: Opening Our Eyes to Invisible People

"Rohadi Nagassar is both fearless and gentle. You're either scared for your life or grateful for his (or both equally). Either way, his words invite you to legitimately examine your place, your truths, and your journey. *When We Belong* is just like him—fearless and gentle. The transformation available when you read it is liberating. So embrace the parts you want to run away from and enjoy the belonging in these pages. I did. And I'm better for it."

**CARLOS A. RODRÍGUEZ,** founder and CEO of The Happy Givers

"In *When We Belong*, Rohadi Nagassar explores ideas connected to belonging, oppression, and freedom with beautiful writing, astute truth-telling, and ardent hope. This book will be a kind companion for Christians on the periphery of the church and a helpful guide for those who aren't."

**CHARLOTTE DONLON,** spiritual director and author of *The Great Belonging: How Loneliness Leads Us to Each Other*

"Belonging is an open door that gives us a warm welcome. It allows us to enter without any hidden agendas or judgment. We are accepted as we are and loved unconditionally. *When We Belong* gives us a panoramic view on the importance of belonging in faith communities, which are often discriminatory, exclusive, and inequitable."

**REV. GRICEL MEDINA, OWS,** pastor, speaker, church planter, and advocate

"Rohadi Nagassar's *When We Belong* explores the idea of belonging in all its twenty-first-century complexity. It is a personal journey and does not attempt to offer an easy answer but casts a vision for belonging that does not lead to more division or to some new grand master plan. It is the story of a very human journey of belonging within the land where one finds oneself."

**REV. DR. RAY ALDRED,** director of the Indigenous Studies Program at the Vancouver School of Theology

"*When We Belong* takes a sobering and spirited look at a way of being that simply ain't right. Leaning into the necessity and reality of deconstruction, this book confronts the diverging paths of resignation and liberation. The result is an image of a belonging that frees us all to be well."

**R. G. A. "TREY" FERGUSON III,** founding president of RFX Ministries, director of equipping at Refuge Church Miami, and cohost of *Three Black Men* podcast

"From deconstruction to atonement theory to institutionalization, Rohadi Nagassar pastorally and prophetically leads the reader through the systemic and systematic barriers of holistic belonging, which he knows intimately. With sights set on a reverberating ancient-yet-present hope, he shows us that true belonging can only come from inclusive belonging, where Christ-permeated radical mutuality of LGBTQIA people, BIPOC people, disabled people, and women can offer the prophetic imagination the church so glaringly needs today. I'm deeply grateful for this book, and hopeful for the church that listens."

**GENA RUOCCO THOMAS,** speaker and author of *Separated by the Border: A Birth Mother, a Foster Mother, and a Migrant Child's 3,000-Mile Journey*

"Topics like deconstruction, reconstruction, and decolonization are heady and emotional for white Christians looking to dismantle white supremacy, and for BIPOC Christians looking to reclaim spiritual practices. Rohadi Nagassar's *When We Belong* surfaces difficult questions for those looking for belonging and challenges us to ask those questions of ourselves and our communities."

**BLAKE CHASTAIN,** host of the *Exvangelical* and *Powers & Principalities* podcasts and writer of The Post-Evangelical Post newsletter

"In this book, Rohadi Nagassar lays out information about the barriers to belonging in the church. By deconstructing and reclaiming church history, Bible interpretation, and contextual spirituality, he argues that authentic belonging and flourishing can be achieved."

**ANGIE HONG,** writer, worship leader, and cofounder of Kinship Commons

# WHEN WE BELONG

# ROHADI
# NAGASSAR

# WHEN WE BELONG

### RECLAIMING
### CHRISTIANITY
*on the*
### MARGINS

**HERALD**
P R E S S

Harrisonburg, Virginia

*To you, dear reader. A remarkable person on the fringe.*

Herald Press
PO Box 866, Harrisonburg, Virginia 22803
www.HeraldPress.com

Library of Congress Cataloging-in-Publication Data
Names: Nagassar, Rohadi, author.
Title: When we belong : reclaiming Christianity on the margins / by Rohadi
    Nagassar.
Description: Harrisonburg, Virginia : Herald Press, [2022] | Includes
    bibliographical references.
Identifiers: LCCN 2022007490 (print) | LCCN 2022007491 (ebook) | ISBN
    9781513810355 (paper) | ISBN 9781513810362 (hc) | ISBN 9781513810379
    (ebook)
Subjects: LCSH: Church and minorities. | Belonging (Social psychology) |
    Social integration--Religious aspects--Christianity. | Marginality,
    Social--Religious aspects--Christianity. | Church membership. | BISAC:
    RELIGION / Christian Living / Social Issues | RELIGION / Christian
    Living / Personal Growth
Classification: LCC BV639.M56 N33 2022  (print) | LCC BV639.M56  (ebook) |
    DDC 254/.5089--dc23/eng/20220325
LC record available at https://lccn.loc.gov/2022007490
LC ebook record available at https://lccn.loc.gov/2022007491

Study guides are available for many Herald Press titles at www.HeraldPress.com.

WHEN WE BELONG
© 2022 by Herald Press, Harrisonburg, Virginia 22803. 800-245-7894.
    All rights reserved.
Library of Congress Control Number: 2022007490
International Standard Book Number: 978-1-5138-1035-5 (paperback);
    978-1-5138-1036-2 (hardcover); 978-1-5138-1037-9 (ebook)
Printed in United States of America

Unless otherwise noted, scripture text is quoted from the *COMMON ENGLISH BIBLE*. Copyright © 2011 COMMON ENGLISH BIBLE. All rights reserved. Used by permission. (www.CommonEnglishBible.com).

26 25 24 23 22                    10 9 8 7 6 5 4 3 2 1

# Contents

# Foreword

IN *ALL ABOUT LOVE*, author bell hooks writes, "The heart of justice is truth telling, seeing ourselves and the world the way it is rather than the way we want it to be."

In *When We Belong*, Rohadi Nagassar courageously leans into the heart of justice: truth-telling. Through vulnerable stories, difficult questions, and a vision for the future of Christianity, Rohadi invites us into the work of asking why the world is the way it is and what we might do about it.

We are living in an important time. Conversations on identity, spirituality, and justice ebb and flow throughout history, and here we are again, charged with the task of bringing truth to these conversations—especially this one, which centers those on the margins of what empirical Christianity has become in the United States and Canada.

In my book *Native: Identity, Belonging, and Rediscovering God*, I write about how the church wants "what is white in me, but not what is Native in me." As an Indigenous woman, I am constantly on a journey of asking where I belong, and whether there *is anywhere to belong* within institutional Christianity. What I wrote in *Native* reminds me of what Rohadi writes:

"How our world works, and how the church operates too, is built around barriers that prevent us from being whole."

Once we name this truth, seeing the world the way it *is*, as hooks taught us, what's next? We don't just talk about it, but enter into the work of allowing ourselves the time to process, grieve, and ask what's next.

I don't fully know the answer to what is next or how the church can fix what has been broken again and again through complicity with white supremacy and colonialism, but when I read books like this one, I know that it's okay to keep asking. So many people are *wondering if and how they might belong*, and instead of making them feel bad for asking, this book reminds us that we should be demanding safe, truly inclusive spaces that are working toward decolonization every step of the way.

As authors, we are always asked to identify the target audience of our books, and that can be difficult to answer. I cannot speak for Rohadi's experience with this, but there are a few different types of people that I certainly hope will read this book. First, those in the process of deconstructing should read it. Second, those who villainize deconstruction should read it. Third, those who object to white supremacy and its tendrils in society should read it, and fourth, those who don't think white supremacy is a real problem should read it.

Wherever you fall into those categories, I'd ask that you hold a few things as you read this book.

First, hold space. Hold space for the truth, for your own story, for space to grieve and accept that things are not as they should be.

Second, hold care and understanding for what you read, and don't try to defend anything. We learn new ways of understanding by first unlearning the old ways. Let yourself unlearn some things, and don't be afraid of letting them go.

Third, hold your questions as dreams for a better way forward. Rohadi offers visions of what beautiful, kinship-oriented community could be throughout this book, and I invite you to dream alongside those visions. Get a journal or a document going, let your entire being imagine what a safe space might feel like, and don't give up on either creating it or finding it for yourself.

Now, onward, toward the journey of finding and owning our sacred belonging.

—Kaitlin Curtice
Poet and award-winning author of *Native: Identity, Belonging, and Rediscovering God*

# Prologue

**LOCKDOWN.** Social distancing. Anti-maskers. Antiracism. Some of the prominent words and phrases we learned as COVID-19 proliferated across the globe in 2020. Like churning seas that expose a lost shipwreck, the global pandemic has revealed hidden features in society too. Realities lying dormant for decades and even centuries. It reveals the skeletons of full-blown inequality rooted in the foundations of society. Features like inherited power and authority in cherished institutions. Economic systems based on land theft, slavery, and exploitation. Racialized hierarchies where white skin is right skin. Gender differences that operate under the commands of patriarchy. These power structures form the foundations of society, but as they become exposed, we discover a facade built on sand. The ground is shifting to reveal cultures and systems bent on constraining people on the margins from reaching their full potential. Do you feel it too?

We begin our journey here because it provides a rare moment in history when nearly every person on the globe can situate themselves on a similar playing field. We all faced varying degrees of loss as death entered our lives. Loss. Now there's a word we're too familiar with. We lost time together with friends and family. We lost a sense of security, and some lost their jobs. Some lost their health, and others lost someone they love. Throughout this unfolding chaos I kept repeating one specific phrase over and over as the days turned into months and then into years: *It's not supposed to be this way*.

The world was falling apart in more ways than one. As the severity of COVID-19 quickly became apparent, adopting precautions and implementing widespread public health recommendations was inconsistent at best. Governments at all levels struggled to provide clear and effective communication on best practices. Although an initial lockdown happened early in March 2020, it didn't last. Then widespread adoption of mask-wearing was slow to roll out, and was met with confusing mandates and coupled with defiant opposition. White supremacists, science deniers, and conspiracy theorists chucked severity aside and banded together to catalyze the exponential and unmitigated spread of the virus. The impact? The death toll attributed to COVID-19 before this book went to press: over 38,000 in Canada; 980,000 in the United States; 166,000 in the United Kingdom; 6.15 million worldwide and counting. (It was a sobering exercise to update these totals during every round of book edits.) These were never the effects of "just another flu."

But the toll doesn't stop there. We don't know the lasting impact of pandemic life. Tallies of suicides, the deterioration of mental health, deaths resulting from inadequate care when hospitals overflowed, and permanent injuries suffered by Long-COVID survivors are currently unknown. It was also the least among us, including people who are poor or disabled, the elderly in care homes, and visible minorities, who took the brunt of the devastation. The term *visible minority* is often used in Canada to describe Black, Indigenous, and other people of color (BIPOC). Although acronyms are imperfect, I will employ two throughout this book: BIPOC, as already described, and LGBTQIA (to include lesbian, gay, bisexual, transgender, queer, intersex, and asexual people.)

Wherever you live, whatever your job, however much money you have, we all share some form of longing to be *liberated* from the pandemic. But that's where the similarities end. We all long for liberation, but liberation is not available to all in the same way. The often quoted phrase "We're all in the same storm, but not in the same boat" acknowledges that catastrophes magnify disparities. That's why it bothers me to hear someone say, "I can't wait to return to normal." The old "normal" is broken and people on the margins of society have no interest in returning to it. The pandemic may have heightened awareness of systemic inequalities, but it turns out that where you're from, what you do, and how much money you have matters a great deal.

Where you live determines access to healthcare. Your job dictates whether you can work from home, set your own hours to care for children, or rush out to get a vaccine at a moment's notice. Your bank account determines how many jobs you need, whether you ride transit to get groceries, or if you have to continue working even when sick. The pandemic exposed more inequalities, pulling them into the light and leaving society at a crossroads. Do we contend with all that ain't right? Or do we aimlessly return to pre-pandemic norms by burying all the exposed wounds for a little while longer?

June 2020 pulled our attention as reverberating calls for justice rose from the streets. The catalyst was three crushing words: "I . . . can't . . . breathe . . ." The murder of George Floyd came on the heels of the similarly high-profile murders of Breonna Taylor and Ahmaud Arbery. Sadly, a much longer list of Black trans lives lost during the same time period never garnered national attention. In Canada, a tenth of the population of the United States, police killed six Indigenous people during the same time frame. A renewed movement sprang up. An emerging generation of voices, led by Black Lives Matter leaders across the globe, made initial demands: dismantle systems that perpetuate anti-Blackness and defund the police. As the reach and size of protests grew, the message sounded familiar. It's a call that's been echoing in the background of society for generations. The civil rights movement in the 1960s was the climactic event of the last century. In this one, new voices oppose the same entrenched systems of injustice and white supremacy. Social media, along with pent-up pandemic angst, mobilized Black voices, only this time joined by Indigenous, Latino, Asian, and a contingent of white people, demanding change. The lingering message is this: *It doesn't have to be this way.*

This raises a necessary follow-up question: Where can we find liberation? This is where I situate this book. *When We Belong* describes new language and pathways that point to a more beautiful way for all people. It provides permission to voice all that ain't right in the world while we embrace new rhythms for life worth living. This journey will take us from individual experiences to questioning cultural systems and church institutions that seek to make those on the margins less whole. Contained herein is a guide to locate a renewed way of being with new possibilities toward wholeness. Here, you will find a reclamation of a dream where the new normal employs a reorientation where the last shall be first, and the first last.

PART I

# ON BELONGING

# 1

# The Search for Belonging

**THERE'S A PECULIAR THING** about belonging: we all need it but it's just so hard to find.

Do you resonate with the struggle to find true belonging? As if only shreds of belonging are accessible, requiring secret passcodes or special fees for entry? Have you noticed that when you happen to acquire a taste of belonging, it dissipates into a mere temporary occasion of "just fitting in"? Is that enough to fill the emptiness? Or do we need deeper ways to belong despite a world designed to consistently exclude?

Rather than ensuring that belonging is available to all, our society is rooted in foundational barriers. Divisions that determine who's in and who will be pushed to the margins. People like me, who aren't white, understand that one of the primary divisions is race. Visible minorities share a deep connection generated from a common suffering and subjugation under the structures of white supremacy. We are reminded daily, and know the feeling in our bones, that finding true belonging will always be elusive.

Ironically, encountering barriers to belonging is a revelation of sorts that would otherwise go unnoticed. Previously disguised features in a world specifically built to marginalized select bodies become known as we encounter them. When we name these hidden pieces, the systems, the cultures, and the beliefs that seek to make us less whole, we begin to tear down the dividing wall. Naming divisions, questioning old ways, and embarking on new paths also has a name: deconstruction. In this way, deconstruction is a pathway unto liberation from all that ain't right in the world. It's a process of finding a more beautiful way to belong and live in the fullness of who we are made to be.

Where to find true belonging is the big question. It can feel too big at times and too daunting to even start. So let's add some framework and bring it closer to home, or closer to faith as it were. You are most likely here because some aspect, or perhaps the whole, of your faith has impinged on your ability to grasp belonging and wholeness in full. In other words, Christianity has become an impediment to finding true belonging. That's a bold claim, but I know some readers are nodding their head in immediate agreement. People pushed to the margins know. We don't need an explanation to describe the harm and trouble we've encountered in the church, both within the institution and with the people. Just as we name features hidden in society preventing our full belonging, so we must do the same for the church.

What are the impediments?

Is it a particular denomination or church? Just a tradition or two? A particular theology? Or is it the whole thing?

For churches located in the West, and the traditions they come from, the answer is more pieces than we care to admit.

It's difficult to lump all churches into a single monolith, although we often try when we use the term "the church." It generally evokes a picture of the dominant variety. There are of course many different traditions, but the differences are only known to insiders. Therefore, to begin, when I refer to "the church," I will maintain the norm. I'm thinking of a body that includes most of what we would consider mainstream Christianity. The major denominations like Roman Catholic, Anglican, Methodist, Baptist, some Orthodox churches, traditions like evangelicalism, some Pentecostalism, and any others with European roots. Within this grouping there are enough similarities to warrant lumping them together. So, what do they have in common?

## CHURCH IMPEDIMENTS

Churches create a finely tuned orchestration of belonging. Assimilation to dominant ways of being and thinking are an expectation. Are you familiar with the struggle? When I asked whether you've ever struggled with belonging, chances are you can pinpoint a situation or two, or three, or six hundred. It happens when our bodies and souls can no longer endure destructive messages and incongruent beliefs. For many, receiving blows to our convictions and personhood accumulates to the point that only one healthy choice remains—leave.

I get it. Some of us are just hanging on. I see you. In the midst of our experience one thing should remain consistent: we ought to trust what we feel in our body and spirit. As someone who's grown up in and been shaped and formed by white evangelicalism, and who even went to seminary, I know there's not a lot of life available without assimilation. This is not the way things ought to be.

When you don't fit, you're pushed to the margins. How does this happen? The primary separation between the margins and the center is the standard of whiteness. Marginalized bodies are dictated by the characteristics determined by the white heteronormative gaze. When you don't adhere to the constantly shifting demands of whiteness you wind up steps behind. This is not because of a lack of effort or any decision of your own, but rather because one of those hidden obstructions to belonging is being unearthed. The primary structural and interpersonal intersections contributing to marginalization are race and gender. We will focus on race predominantly in this book, but there are other important divisions, including sexuality, disability, neurodiversity, ethnicity, class, nationality, and so on.

The idea that Christianity is an impediment to living out your whole being sounds like the opposite of what it should be. In theory the Christian faith is a grand narrative, from Genesis to Revelation, about God on a mission to bring the world into right relationship. It's a dream designed to liberate us from all that ain't right in the world. From all the despair of a pandemic, all the way down to how we belong to ourselves. It may be expressed through a community practicing radical hospitality, inclusivity, unity in diversity, justice, and the pursuit of wholeness in mind, body, and spirit. Sound good so far?

Sure, it's hard to reflect every one of these attributes. After all, the church is full of people and we are a flawed bunch. I am, however, dismayed by how many churches define themselves by the barriers they preserve over the freedom they should announce. It is not a freedom tainted by the aspirations of Western individualism. Rather, it is a promised dream where we can live out our whole and authentic selves. Yet true belonging in churches seems out of reach even for the insiders.

That's the other reason why you're here. You've grown up in, or have otherwise been shaped and formed by, a particular way of believing and understanding the world. And then something went awry. Beliefs, ideas, opinions called into question as they became obstacles preventing full belonging and human flourishing. A version of faith that leaves a gnawing feeling that there's more to life than what's on the inside. What we lack to make sense of our search and move forward is the language to name the problem and ultimately locate a life-giving alternative.

## FINDING THE RIGHT WORDS

I remember a conversation with my friend Lis[1] on the subject of patriarchy in the Bible. She had recently read *The Making of Biblical Womanhood* by professor Beth Allison Barr. "That book finally gave me the language to describe the problems with 'biblical womanhood,' that what I knew deep down inside wasn't right," Lis said. When we lack the right vocabulary to name what we're feeling, we often get stuck. Sometimes for a long time. Without the right words, we may struggle to identify why we feel at odds with ourselves. An unidentifiable piece of our being strikes a dissonant chord filled with wrong notes we can't shake. If we ignore it, we stagnate, burying a voice within ourselves longing to be free. To fill in the blanks we need a renewed hope to confirm the nagging sensation—call it belief—that better is out there. If you wish, you can even call it promptings from the Spirit of God trying to set the captive part of you free.

New vocabulary helps imagine new ways of being and belonging. It offers form to shape a faith that exists beyond the baggage of institutions and their boundaries of belonging. This is not to say we throw away all history and tradition.

But it does mean permission to conduct a deep introspection of core beliefs, including where they come from. Some of us need permission to do this work because we've learned that the wrong question can push us to the margins. But you may already know that. You are already questioning the ways you were formed to believe. You are asking why your brand of Christianity struggles with compassion, justice, radical inclusion, and the love for the other and the enemy. Why is preserving traditions or appointing gatekeepers to determine who is worthy enough to enter community a paramount concern? I'm with you. I don't want this brand of Christianity either, because if the "right" version of Christianity is a religion built to associate with the powers of Western thought and empire, then the entire faith from cross, resurrection, and ultimate restoration lacks power and meaning. To quote pastor Mika Edmondson, "When society has its knee on your neck, you need a God who will deliver souls *and bodies*."[2] We need more than salvation for privileged souls disconnected from the plight of the world, a salvation that escapes this world for heaven in the clouds. No, we need a redemptive story for all of creation in the here and now.

Thankfully, this hope exists, and it specifically includes those on the margins. We have a unique and intimate connection with Jesus and his hope of good news *now*. I see this relationship emerge when I read stories in the Bible. I am drawn to the ways the last become first, how the meek and the hopeless inherit the earth, how those who thirst for justice will find fulfillment, and those who show mercy will receive mercy. These are all essential characteristics and teachings of Jesus Christ and simultaneously the source to find true belonging. I argue that these stories are worth reclaiming because, like you, I'm tired of struggling to find community in order to be whole. Tired of the exhaustive and elusive search for a church to not just "get by," but flourish too. Tired of giving up a piece of myself to just fit in.

I stopped running into these deadends nearly twenty years ago. Something in me said, Enough! There's got to be a better way. And despite a lifetime of trying to fit in, despite seeing how marginalized people are intentionally kept on the margins, I carry a deep faith. Despite twenty years shaped in mainstream evangelicalism (my experience is translatable to most other traditions), I've also spent the past twenty years leading church expressions outside of the institution. I have great hope for the church but no vested interest in preserving the institution. We can reject bad teachings in full. That includes ones that have formed beliefs in generations and for centuries, to reclaim good news that seeks to make us whole. Finding this path to ultimate wholeness is the journey before us now. One rooted in a Christian faith that embodies Jesus toward a more whole and liberated existence in community and place. It's the pursuit of freedom from all that ain't right in the world, and the reclamation of true belonging.

# 2

# Grasping True Belonging

*Oahu, Hawaii.*

I sink my toes deeper into a powder of white sand as the sun begins to set. A barely there breeze whispers past my body as blue skies shift to deep orange and pink hues. They linger above darkening yet calm waters. In the distance, a sailboat bobs along the ocean surface, and just as the sun touches the horizon, the two meet and the ship is briefly contained within the glowing orange orb. Deep breath. Exhale. Something in my soul knows that this space and this moment, on the traditional lands of the Kanaka Maoli, is a piece of heaven on earth. Our bodies have an intuitive connection to the land to spot and appreciate beauty, don't they?

*Kananaskis, Alberta.*

I'm standing at the base of a mountain as my head tilts to the summit. Three thousand feet and six hours of hiking await. Leaving the sound of the roadway behind, I plod toward the top, step by step by step. I'm carrying a pack with extra clothes (the weather can change on a dime), hiking poles (for my knees on the way down), my camera (the one you hold with two hands), a handheld compass and a GPS (I don't know how to use either), lots of water and lunch (ham and Swiss), and some bear spray (in case I'm about to become lunch).

There's something both alluring and therapeutic in reconnecting with the land by spending hours bathing in a Rocky Mountain forest completely alone. Hiking without any outside distractions or interactions is sublime. Just me in my head where I like to be. It's also a chance to listen for any whispering voice from God or the trees. I usually don't leave disappointed. The last part of why bother trouncing up a relentless hill has to do with the mental challenge, coupled with a side of danger. To conquer a peak and see the world—just for a moment—from the very top is worth the turmoil. Little about this exercise is about, well, the exercise.

I maintain a steady pace for the first hour. The incline steepens and will do so until I reach the summit. The higher I go the thinner the air gets. After hour two, then three, I start to question my resolve as my legs grow weary. Why am I doing this to myself? I notice a thinning patch of moss cushioned in a rock crevice as I catch my breath while leaning against my poles. I don't even like hiking. The doubt and pain begin to creep in, but are met with more steps up and upward. The last five hundred feet are the hardest. I can see the summit but it's not getting any closer, which intensifies the desire to quit. My pace slows to a crawl on all fours as I traverse tricky rock outcroppings. No point turning back now. With one hundred feet left, my excitement returns. This is the part where the view opens and the sight becomes . . . magic. I stretch out my hand to touch the clouds. Just a little further now . . .

Few things are as exhilarating as standing on a mountaintop. At this height the view extends further than my vision can comprehend. I celebrate by letting out a scream of both triumph and despair that gets lost in grey rock abyss below. Up here things are different. I am fully alive with nobody around me to tell me otherwise.

*My dining room.*

It took a few trips to the grocery store, but I'm ready. Five pounds of beef (eye of round cut thin by the butcher), fancy breads, and pretty much every vegetable that can be skewered on a prong and then dipped in a pot. Every fall I hold a fondue evening for friends. Two pots of broth sit over open flames as guests cook their choice of foods. I like fondue evenings because they are intentionally slow. It's a tradition on top of my enjoyment to cook with and for friends. The meal lasts for hours as conversations fill the void. This time someone jumps straight into the deep end: "Do you think God exists despite all the evil in the world?" Smiles break out as the discussion intensifies. It's these moments, when everyone is connected and engaged, that feel special. I remind myself to take note, remember the people, the aromas, and in particular how my body feels. I feel good. Immersed and cherishing a moment to just be me in my own skin. A grin widens across my face as I sense the affirmation: These are my people—I belong here . . .

When was the last time you inhabited belonging in your entire being? When you heard the heartbeat of the land as the perfect sunset unfolded? When you shared communion with others and felt fully seen? When you sensed freedom in your own body? It's a tricky question because it presumes you *don't* have belonging in all its pieces now. But belonging should be abundant, available to all so we may flourish and be whole. In fact, I want a *life* that shares and emanates substantive presence within enduring belonging. One that embodies characteristics like love, justice, beauty, and hope. But for many of us, belonging remains sporadic or constantly out of reach. It's not supposed to be this way. Which raises the necessary follow-up question: What way should it be? Belonging is out there; I just wish it weren't so hard to find. Let's go searching.

## THE SEARCH FOR TRUE BELONGING

In the search for true belonging, I want to name the features that ultimately liberate my whole being. I want pieces that contribute to lasting depth over a lifetime, rather than fleeting moments in the present. Oftentimes, however, that's all we can find. We consume the lowest-hanging fruit of commodified belonging that preys upon our need to fill ourselves with outside affirmations. Sometimes we seek any semblance of belonging to stave off the alternative—loneliness—unable to see the two as companions rather than adversaries.[1] It's no surprise that prepackaged offerings are insufficient to fill our longings. So what are the options for deeper connection?

In her book *Braving the Wilderness*, Brené Brown explores belonging rooted in her own story and research. Her pursuit was catalyzed by these words from the great Maya Angelou: "You only are free when you realize you belong no place— you belong every place—no place at all."[2] The phrase contains an incisive authenticity coupled with a tinge of emptiness. It also strikes me as stilted and disjointed. I've gone back to reread the full transcript of Angelou's interview, and have even watched the recording, trying to locate additional meaning hidden in her voice or cadence, but to no avail. Her words remain powerfully perplexing. They also leave me feeling as though I haven't fully absorbed the wisdom hidden in the paradox. Parts of it I grasp right away. Who better understands belonging nowhere than racialized minorities pushed to the

margins of society? I don't belong anywhere, because I don't
match the characteristics of a dominant archetypal body—in
our context, the white heteronormative male. But Angelou
couples belonging nowhere with belonging everywhere. That's
the part I don't get. Maybe I'm not supposed to. Perhaps a hint
of lingering tension is the point. I can live with that. But it does
strike me as sad that when asked "Where do you belong?," the
answer would be "No place at all." Maybe I haven't worked
out a professional understanding of belonging. Perhaps I don't
belong enough to myself? I shudder to think I've missed both
the big question and the answer.

Brown leans in and, leveraging her research, offers
her insight.

> True belonging is the spiritual practice of believing in and
> belonging to yourself so deeply that you can share your
> most authentic self with the world and find sacredness in
> both being a part of something and standing alone in the
> wilderness. True belonging doesn't require you to *change*
> who you are; it requires you to *be* who you are.[3]

And now I'm stuck again. I struggle with the notion that
we can belong everywhere so long as we belong to ourselves. It
strikes me as an individualistic answer in a world that mistak-
enly admires the demands of rugged individualism. The other
part of my aversion to belonging everywhere is again filtered
through my experience as a racialized minority.

I remember when white people excitedly championed
Brené Brown's ideas when they first came out. They declared,
"I belong everywhere!," which never sat right with me. I still
can't wrap my head around the idea that belonging is determined by the individual. This posture honestly strikes me as
colonial. White people are culturally formed by a history that

says they can belong anywhere by quietly leveraging privilege built on conquest. There's a lot of inherited power bestowed on the self that can belong anywhere. Brown doesn't have much to say about this. In fact, that's one of the glaring weaknesses in her work—she has little to say about race and how it may influence her work and shape her studies. But then I'm reminded of Angelou's words, and think of another author, Sebene Selassie.

Selassie writes about belonging in her book *You Belong: A Call for Connection*. She's also a Buddhist teacher, which I find doubly interesting since her faith differs from my own and provides new insight. She writes, "The key to belonging is within. Belonging is my nature: therefore, I belong everywhere and so does everyone else."[4] Her picture of belonging seems rooted within as well. She does add a Buddhist teaching called the doctrine of two truths to her argument. "Belonging flourishes within this paradox: everything is connected, yet everything is experienced as separate."[5] Connection implies we can't do life alone, that there's an innate need for others in conjunction with the self. We need each other. I get it. The brief pandemic lockdowns around March 2020 proved that. But Selassie's approach still remains rooted within the self. To me there are some missing pieces.

It's important to note neither Brown nor Selassie argue that you can make it on your own. Selassie speaks to humanity's shared connectivity as a grounding point to belonging. Brown articulates the need for community. Both include these additional components, but they maintain a foundation of belonging rooted in the self. This is the tension I hold to the wisdom of Brown, Selassie, and Angelou: true belonging is not rooted exclusively in me. The notion that we belong everywhere so long as we discover what Brown calls the "authentic self" is incomplete. If we were to measure belonging in terms of health, it's not in the self where we find whole health, but rather within relationships found in abundant community.[6]

Don't get me wrong. Ironically, I believe one of the building blocks to belonging is discovering the authentic self. Parts of this book will dig into the importance of personal identity. It's a crucial step toward wholeness. I have also lived what Brown calls the "wilderness experience"; when the authentic self stands in opposition to expected cultural norms and assumptions. Being true to your convictions may inevitably pit you against the world (or the church). Not "the world" as in the land, or what is spatially around you, but those unwritten and constantly changing standards of how to be seen fully. We can't rely on these outside affirmations, because they are fleeting and potentially destructive. We can't root our identity in the ways we might belong *to* something. But what if true belonging is found in how we belong *with* something?

Picture a vast forest. If the self is the center of belonging, then it would be the roots of a single tree. Spirituality and community are the branches or leaves. Here's the problem. A tree can lose a limb—let's say its spirituality—yet still retains all the necessary components to grow uninhibited and healthy. But the same can't be said about belonging. Even when you belong to yourself, you still need connection or spirituality, not as mere additions, but as central components of the whole. Rather than thinking of true belonging as the roots of a single tree, take a step back and look at the entire environment. Trees need other trees to share root structures. They need sun, soil, and water to survive and multiply. An ecosystem is working in harmony to create a healthy habitat. Therefore, it is the *relationship* between all of these things that makes the tree, in the forest, whole. We can't compartmentalize essential elements of belonging, because they're all supposed to be joined together.

Brown and Selassie certainly acknowledge the importance of the environment, including love and connection. The difference is, I'm pulling away from the focus on that single tree. (Isn't there a saying of "can't see the forest for the trees"?) We are not only material bodies. Philosopher Jacques Ellul writes that if we "sustain the body without feeding the whole being, everything will suffer."[7] Shifting from the self as the center of true belonging is certainly a challenge, as it questions the heart of Western individualism, which asserts that the individual is seated at the center of one's own material universe. It also displaces the notion that individuals can be separated into spirit and matter. All of this means that the search for a holistic understanding of true belonging resides not in individualism, or even in how individual parts contribute to the whole, but rather in how the whole can be described in relationship to its different parts. It's the discovery of how we belong *with* something*s*.

## A WHOLE APPROACH TO BELONGING

My approach to true belonging isn't mine at all, but rather appeals to the basic foundations of the Christian faith. The two primary sources I will reference are found in the gospel of Matthew and the gospel of John. Before we take a closer look, we must acknowledge what might be a place of disconnection for some. You might be in the midst of questioning whether the stories in the Bible are trustworthy enough to serve as suitable foundations in your life. I argue that yes, there are inextricable pieces in the stories that contribute to our wholeness, and they are worth reclaiming. But I don't want to assume that you are in this place. Chances are, if you are struggling with putting together broken pieces of belief and past church experiences, you know the words but question whether they can be trusted.

The purpose of this book is to reclaim pathways unto collective liberation. You must embark on your own journey to get to a place of trust and beauty again. This will make more sense as we continue this adventure together, but know that at the start, there may be some dissonance.

In Matthew 22:35–40, Jesus replies to a trick question about the most important law. He says, "You must love the Lord your God with all your heart, with all your being, and with all your mind. This is the greatest commandment. The second is: You must love your neighbor as yourself" (my adaptation of the CEB). In John 13:34–35, the scene narrows to a dinner table with close friends . . . Jesus declares, "I give you a new commandment: Love each other. Just as I have loved you, so you also must love each other. This is how everyone will know that you are my disciples, when you love each other."

Jesus is sharing foundations for his followers, and the world, to embody—to love in all its forms. Love reveals the exciting possibilities that help situate a move to reclaim a renewed Christianity, describe true belonging, and find our ultimate liberation unto wholeness. Digging deeper reveals more connections. For instance, neither commandment is separated into three, four, or five different commandments. Each is presented as one. The greatest commandment in Matthew has multiple parts that all contribute to make a whole.

When we look closer at the love commandments, we see a profound range. To begin in Matthew, the first focus of our love is devoted to God. What this looks like is only—yet profoundly—described by what's behind the action: love with our entire beings, our entire hearts, and our entire minds. Note the connection here. From the onset of the great commandment, and its application to a more whole picture of true belonging, the self is drawn into immediate relationship.

Jesus then takes the idea further. The whole expands to focus on a love devoted to the neighbor. Not mere connectivity with others, but a vital and deep inclusion emanating from the love we reciprocate with God. Now the relationship has two parts, God and the neighbor. But we're not done. There's a third part in Matthew's gospel that looks inward, where Brown and Selassie focus, to the self. Our love of God and of our neighbor are reflections of how much we love ourselves. Sometimes we forget this part. Sometimes it's because we don't know how. . . . Nonetheless, the relationship between these parts contribute to a wholistic approach to true belonging. But we're still not done. There's one more piece found in John.

John 13 is thick with tension and emotion. The synoptic gospels (Matthew, Mark, and Luke) include Christ's reinterpretation of the shared meal, from which churches derive the sacrament of communion. John doesn't include the bread, the wine, and the wine once more; rather, he replaces the story with the "sacrament" of footwashing. No doubt the disciples are both uneasy of and alert to the significance of the evening, especially when Jesus shares about his imminent crucifixion. Initially, the disciples reject the premise. Rather than assuage their mounting concern, Jesus adds that not only is he going to die, but one of the disciples will betray him. The meal ends with a final reinterpretation of commandments. A new commandment is brought forward: Love one another. It isn't so much new as it is definitive in the object. This time it's love for one another.

True belonging and wholeness are found in how we relate to one another and our neighbor in love; how we relate to God and the hope for this world; and how we relate to ourselves. It's a love that's embodied. A choice that must be lived out, attempted, experienced, received, and imperfectly pursued.

Embodied means to literally enflesh. To make visible the connections to the senses usually with physical presence. It's those down-to-earth places where we get our hands dirty. Earth. Place. Those two words refer to the land we situate ourselves on. It's a constant wherever we live. Our understanding of land and place, however, takes on different meanings depending on cultural formation. Our Western understanding of land use is filtered through the ideology of capitalism. To subdue, conquer, and ultimately own land. As we appeal toward a reclamation of belonging, and a faith venturing for the same, we must reach for a different set of principles. A philosophy of life that lives in harmony with the land and its indigenous inhabitants, including animal, bird, and human.[8] Land is foundation because it's the foundation we walk upon. That makes it an obvious component to belonging because just as we can relate to God and to other humans, so we are also invited to experience and relate to the land. To cultivate relationship over consistent exploitation.

True belonging is a path towards flourishing and is found when we holistically embody love with one another and the other; how we love God; how we love ourselves; and how we relate to the lands we are situated on. Each part is connected and integral to the whole. This is our framework to move forward. Now we need to fill in the blanks, learning as we go and developing practical examples of what new and reclaimed possibilities look like. Remember, the thing about belonging is that it's just so hard to find. We need liberation from all that seeks to make us less whole by naming barriers and impediments undermining our pursuit.

# 3

# The Problems with Belonging

**THE ACCLAIMED,** and now longest running, television show *The Simpsons* launched in December 1989. There are thirty-three seasons and counting, and I think I've seen nearly every episode. It's no surprise I might turn to *The Simpsons* for a metaphor or two.

In season 6, episode 12, Homer Simpson tries to obtain membership into the exclusive Stonecutters society (a fictional portrayal of modern-day Freemasons). Initially, the club refuses him entry, which evokes a painful childhood memory. In the flashback scene, kid Homer is climbing a ladder with other children to enter a backyard treehouse. Each child is welcomed enthusiastically, "Come on in, there's plenty of room!" But when Homer arrives, he's in for a sad surprise.

"Sorry, not you, Homer." The child points to a sign hanging outside the treehouse that reads "No Homers Club."

Kid Homer replies, "But you let in Homer Glumplich!"

The child replies, "[The sign] says no Homers*ssss*. We're allowed to have one."

## FIVE OPTIONS DESCRIBING CHURCH BELONGING

When it comes to diversity, churches are No Homers Clubs. There's a limit to diversity beyond dominant cultural norms, which in turn influences inclusivity. The infamous and often quoted words of Rev. Dr. Martin Luther King still ring true: "It is one of the tragedies of our nation, one of the shameful trage- dies, that eleven o'clock on Sunday morning is one of the most segregated hours, if not the most segregated hours, in Chris- tian America."[1] Today, diversity in congregations or leadership is not a common characteristic in most Western churches. Racial segregation remains one of the primary differentiating factors in churches and represents one of the primary barriers to belonging.[2] But that's only the start.

I believe there are five main categories that describe how belonging works in churches. I will present four of them now, along with examples and explanations. The fifth one I will share later in chapter 10.

### Option 1: Assimilate

Although demographics are shifting, white Protestant and white Catholic traditions are currently the dominant forms of Christianity in the West. A person outside of white able-bod- ied cisgender hegemony is either rejected or, at best, absorbed. Assimilation demands people on the margins adopt the cul- ture, beliefs, and expectations of the center in order to belong. It makes no attempt at reciprocity, which means Christians on the margins must live out a caricature of our true selves in order to fit in. In most instances that means we must adhere to the unwritten rules of whiteness (more on this topic in chapter 5). This poses a conundrum. We can either give up a piece of ourselves by assimilating, or disturb the status quo in search of change. Both come with a cost. The former means losing parts of our identity (or ignoring it for a time). The latter has an expiration date. A time when a token marginalized "pet" takes their advocacy for change too far, and turns into a perceived community "threat."[3] The result is eventual disfellowship or burnout. Although Christians on the margins cover a wide spectrum of diversity, the primary division is what's visible—skin color (or race). This means one can never fully assimilate into white churches if one is not white. This explains a lot of my church experience growing up.

### The absurdities of assimilation

There are certain ways we measure people to determine whether or not they belong. Outward appearance, specifically skin color, is one of the base methods. After the appearance standard, further inquiries follow. Perhaps you've been on the receiving end of them before:

"What are you?"

"So where are you from?"

Two questions I've been asked a million[4] times before. If you are classified as white, then you've probably never received the first one. After all, that would be downright rude. A white woman once tried to explain to me why older white folks typically ask these questions. "It's because they're genuinely curious. They grew up in a world where everyone was white."

I'm sure demographics are a part of it, but that still doesn't excuse the inquiry. What may sound like an innocent question is in fact rooted in prejudice. It reveals how stereotypes are used to determine whether or not someone belongs *here*. Here can mean a church, neighborhood, city, or country. If you're white you get a free, no-questions-asked pass to belong in virtually every public space. That's an inheritance rooted in the spoils of colonization and domination. I can't imagine how Indigenous peoples, the original inhabitants of this land going back millennia, carry the idea of being too "brown" to pass the belonging test.

Ironically, I have deeper roots (and they aren't that old) in Canada than most white people I know. But time doesn't matter. White people automatically belong, and everyone else may be classified as foreign.

It's harder to ascribe barriers that are not physically apparent. Neurodiversity, many disabilities, and sexuality to name a few. If you have an accent (other than an English or Australian accent), you will eventually face the inquisition of belonging, albeit not along racialized lines. If you are visibly disabled, you may be used to harmful attention. If you are a woman, then certain gender assumptions can dictate in which spaces you can belong. If you are queer, then you will always play the guessing game of where you can live out your whole self without abrupt or extreme aggression on your personhood. When it comes to race, there are no exceptions if you aren't white. It's assumed you're not from here, unless "here" is a place where white people are the minority, like inner-city neighborhoods, Chinatown, or Toronto. In regions where there is a history between white and Black and brown bodies on the land, belonging is dictated by assumptions of superiority above all else.

Not looking culturally familiar because I have brown skin presents a number of innate challenges I can't escape. My burden is I have to prove I belong in my own neighborhood with a curated selection of answers tailored to whom I'm interacting with. It might be through language fluency (no slang), how I dress, highlighting common cultural artifacts (I play hockey too), or divulging my perceived wealth (I own a house on this street). If I don't play the game of belonging roulette, the assumption will always be, You're not from here. But even if I do play, social foundations are still shifting beneath my feet, lurking to disrupt my search to belong.

Admittedly, culture is changing. Strangers rarely ask me "What are you?" and "Where are you from?" anymore. But is there ever an appropriate time to ask where someone is from? I can think of only two scenarios. (For you, there's probably only one.) For me I accept "What are you?" from one group of people: Filipinos. Why? Filipinos don't ask me "What are you?" and certainly don't inquire about my appearance as a question of division. Rather, their inquiry is marked by a single word· "Pilipino?" Do you see the difference? Everyone else categorizes me as "other." Filipinos *invite* me into belonging. There's a certain connection when one Filipino discovers another roaming around Canada. For this reason, they're always looking to claim me as one of their own. "Sorry, I'm too tall," I respond, much to their disappointment and mine.

The other appropriate time to ask where someone is from, or what they are, is within the context of relationship as you get to know them better. (I guess the other place would be a census, but I never have a box to tick, so let's ignore it.) This question doesn't happen at first. I would judge you if our first conversation were to include "But seriously, *what are you?*" Secondly, don't guess. For me, you would never get it. Don't try to guess with your friends, and never guess with a stranger. So what should you say when you reach the right moment? Here's a helpful tip. If you're genuinely interested in someone, ask them, "Tell me about your people." Then sit down and listen to the stories. And yes, even white people have ethnicity, so get ready to answer the same question in return.

I mentioned earlier that assimilation contains no expectation of reciprocity. If you're not from the dominant culture, then the assumption is that you will change to fit it, and never the other way around. But here's the stark reality, and there are varying degrees to this as well: *Your root identity can never be assimilated*. What pulls the barriers to belonging into the light, making them visible, is when you add community to the mix.

### Assimilating beliefs and bodies

Are you now, or have you ever been, connected in life-giving faith communities where you can be your whole self without reservation? Or do you too often find yourself on the outside looking in? Have you ever felt weird after a church service or during conversations with Christians? It may have been because of an inappropriate statement about women in ministry or doctrines about queer people. Perhaps it was a casual ableist or racist comment. Maybe it's been outright sexual or spiritual abuse. For that, I'm sorry. These moments are accompanied by a small voice in your heart saying, "That ain't right." Your voice is right. Receive this affirmation: You're not alone.

The unfortunate part with "that ain't right" moments in church communities is how often they represent issues that determine belonging. Support the "wrong" position and you may be ostracized. Raise up an issue that's of little interest to the whole, and your call will be treated as insignificant. That's counter to what we all long for: to be seen in our full authentic selves within life-giving community. *Life-giving* means a place where the longing for liberation and wholeness is shared. The trouble is, communities that do not demand assimilation are just so hard to find. For me, I didn't find one until I started one.

I spent my formative years growing up in what I would now call "white evangelicalism." We were part of a small church in an obscure denomination that met in a community center in the suburbs. Despite our size we shared common features from contemporary evangelicalism, including the key figures we listened to, positions on controversial topics, Bible studies we used, and even the music we sang. And just as it is for American evangelicals, adhering to particular belief systems ranging from theology to politics was a key factor to belonging. Step outside of these boundaries and you're out. Go to church service, say the sinner's prayer, read your Bible, all typical expectations. Then there were select theological issues to consider. The end-times craze generated by the now scorned Left Behind series dominated our imaginations in youth group. Then, just as I was old enough to vote, Canada began the process to legalize same-sex marriage. We were shaped to believe that if the country went forward with the change, hallowed cultural icons like suburban family life would be lost forever. Spoiler alert. Twenty years later the country hasn't fallen apart, although Christian membership has declined.

Right beliefs, however, do not circumvent another need of assimilation— identity. I remember one Sunday morning when my mom and I, with my sister in tow, arrived early to put up chairs for service. One of the elders also showed up early to lend a hand. Setup was moving along swimmingly when, completely unprompted, the elder took his hands, pulled his eyes to become squinty, and said in what I assume was his attempt at a Chinese accent, "Many hands make light work." Mom and I stopped dead in our tracks. Did we just hear that? What was that about?! But in true Japanese fashion, we said nothing, frowned to ourselves, and continued about our task.

Then there was that time during my late teen years when a young couple visited our service for the first time. First off, new people at our church was a shock, but it spurred that evangelical excitement only newcomers can produce. Second, new people my age who weren't white had never happened before. Finally, I rejoiced to myself, more people who look like me. My joy was short lived. They soon departed. We stayed friends, and later they told me why they left. One evening, they had invited the pastor over to share a traditional Sri Lankan meal. Without prompting, he announced with curiosity, "Show us how you people eat with your hands!"

"That ain't right" moments happened even when I was in church leadership. I spent a brief time during seminary interning at a large evangelical church. One year, I was tasked to prepare Easter service. Part of my job was to find multimedia videos to include. I did manage to find an inspirational animation that ended at the empty tomb. The audio was a sermon clip featuring a Black preacher with the emblematic cadence. This will fit great, I thought. To my surprise, when I shared the clip it didn't even generate a conversation. The lead pastor scoffed and immediately shut it down. Why didn't it fit? "Too gospel-y" was his answer. It took me ten years before I connected the dots. In a small-town church where the only Black body was a young boy adopted into a white family, the voice of a traditional Black preacher was off limits.

These are three brief snapshots of many "that ain't right" moments that hounded me wherever I went within white evangelicalism. Maybe I'm an anomaly? Maybe I'm too sensitive to weird events? Or maybe I should stop questioning my experiences. Maybe it's the church that's impeding whole belonging, especially for people on the margins. But you probably already knew that. Or maybe you're just coming to the realization now.

## Option 2: Join an ethnic church

Rather than "white" church (we just call it "church," since only ethnic traditions have the extra moniker), ethnic churches are another option in the search for belonging. Ethnic churches exist because historically white institutional Christianity did not permit full membership to racialized minorities (among other marginalized groups). For example, the African American church emerged as a necessary response to slaveholder Christianity that barred African Americans from participation (or salvation) in white churches. In *The Color of Compromise*, historian Jemar Tisby writes,

> Racial segregation in [white] Christian churches occurred in the eighteenth century in large part because white believers did not oppose the enslavement of African persons. Instead, Christians sought to reform slavery and evangelize the enslaved. In the process, they learned to rationalize the continued existence of slavery. Many white Christians comforted themselves with the myth that slavery allowed them to more adequately care for the material and spiritual needs of enslaved Africans.[5]

Other ethnic traditions were born out of necessity too. The Chinese church is relatively new compared to its institutional African American counterpart, but is similar in the sense that it coalesced because we too were not permitted full membership or belonging in white churches. As a multiethnic person I belong to many ethnicities, but simultaneously none at all. It poses curious problems when it comes to joining ethnic churches.

My first name is Rohadi. Pronounced precisely as it is written. It's Indonesian but I have no personal connection to the country or the people. My dad thought it would be great to name me after a friend he once had. My parents had a backup plan in case Rohadi didn't work out. My middle name is Barry, which is on the opposite end of the "where are you from judging by your name" spectrum. There's no significance behind my middle name, but it contains one important feature: it sounds more "Canadian." I'm a first-generation immigrant born in Trinidad and I now call Canada home. Trinidad is the southernmost island in the Caribbean, sitting just off the coast of Venezuela. My dad and his side of the family are from Trinidad, with roots going back to northern India. Things about Trinidad you should know: its primary export is oil, although it was initially sugarcane; they have avocados (pronounced "zaboca") the size of pineapples; and as my aunts always remind me: once a Trini always a Trini.

My mom was born in Calgary, Alberta. Her mom is Chinese though she never spoke Taishanese. She was too ashamed for a variety of reasons. My grandpa is Japanese, and his family was interned during the Second World War. More on that later. Grandma and Grandpa were born in Canada. Both my Chinese and my Japanese family immigrated to Canada sometime between the Great Wars, which means I have roots on this land going back over a hundred years. I have one younger sister who's fair skinned and can pass as some kind of Asian. I'm darker and can blend in only in few choice places on earth, but usually nowhere at all. That's an unfortunate and consistent problem I have faced my entire life. When I step outside my house, something or somebody will remind me I'm out of place. Part of that is a product of living in a predominantly white neighborhood for nearly fifteen years. We sit on the edge of a more commercial and multiethnic corridor that includes a mini Koreatown and a Walmart. Over the years, stores and even advertisements have shifted to reflect more diversity. I notice them not because I see someone who looks like me on a billboard; rather, *not* seeing a white person initially strikes me as out of place. The same applies to my body not ten blocks away, closer to my home. If I bump into my neighbors while I'm out for a walk, they don't recognize me. In fact, I have to be literally standing in my garage before I'm correctly identified. I suppose that's somewhat of a blessing in this part of Canada. I'd rather have anonymity for being "out of place" than experience being policed.

By ethnicity I am West Indian, Chinese, and Japanese. By nationality I'm Canadian, but could claim Trinidad too (or should, as per my aunties). So where do you think I can belong? West Indian churches tend to be culturally Black Caribbean. I don't fit there, since my ancestors are from India. I'm too dark and don't speak or look Chinese or Japanese enough to seamlessly fit into those churches either. Which leaves multiethnic churches (more on that next) or white churches ("Canadian" churches), but you know the problem there—I'm not white.

For those who can slide into ethnic communities without trouble, the pros include retaining ethnic identity without the pressure of assimilation. Being around your own people produces a certain amount of relief from a world rooted in whiteness. The cons are you have to be a particular ethnicity, and usually in full (at least on the outside) to gain the benefits of full belonging. I remember conversing with a Japanese person who unknowingly othered me by saying, "Oh right, you're Japanese too, I guess, if that's how you want to identify." Biracial people will also know the dance of looking the "right amount" of a certain ethnicity to avoid any jokes about being mixed.

Ethnic exclusivity is understandable, given that minority traditions formed as a resistance against assimilation. But it should raise questions about what the future holds for these churches in terms of embodying full inclusivity. Another con is that younger generations get caught in the tension between two cultures. Younger generations try to rid themselves of archaic religious traditions, search for contemporary expressions of faith, wind up at option 1, last a few years, but return after facing the pressures of assimilation.

## Option 3: Build diversity

The third option, one held in tension, is to join a church in the midst of embracing a more diverse and inclusive community. I know of many churches working hard to tangibly welcome marginalized people. It's work against historical norms. That is to say it's not easy, because it doesn't come naturally. Affirming congregations are one example. The challenge in option 3 churches: diversity to what degree? Because churches in the West are formed in homogeneity, and lack distinct competencies at building more inclusive space, there's always a *diversity limit*. Like the affirming congregation that welcomes queer folks but won't contend with its formation in white supremacy that excludes queer folks who are BIPOC.

The other option is to join already diverse churches. Oftentimes we call these churches multiethnic, but diversity stretches beyond ethnicity into all other intersections as well. Like the fully affirming multiethnic church that reflects diversity, and practices of continually learning from the margins, in congregation and leadership as well. In my search for belonging and watching what new ideas institutional Christianity produces, I have found these kinds of churches to be very rare. Which is sad in many ways. I've always wondered what it would be like to stroll into a church completely unencumbered by the feeling of "you don't belong here." I often try to test this posture of freedom when I visit a new city. Ultimately, something always gets in the way. My French is too broken, and I don't look remotely Parisian, to pass in Paris. I keep looking the wrong way when I cross the street in London. I definitely don't fit in Iceland, and I don't pass for "local" in Calgary, a city I've called home for nearly forty years. Even in Trinidad I don't fit, although if I've had proper sun and I'm wearing sunglasses I will blend in. In fact, the only place in the world where I've been confused for a local (and only momentarily) was Hawaii. Not because I look native Hawaiian, but because there's enough Asian mix on the islands that I was mistaken for a recent transplant. My multiethnic heritage is unique, and locating church spaces where people on the margins can seamlessly belong has eluded me.

Cultivating full inclusive communities is rare and exhausting work. When people in conventional churches try to lead this kind of change, efforts are constantly met by resistance, gaslighting, and minute, incremental shifts at best. Remember, there is at best a limit when expanding belonging in full. Centuries of white supremacy formation cannot be undone through decades of hard work and prayer. Ultimately, there's not a lot of energy or interest to make permanent shifts. So Christians on the margins are right back to where we started in the search for belonging. What usually follows is exhaustion, discouragement, or even walking away from faith entirely.

## Option 4: Leave

In my small part of the world the big news to start 2020 wasn't the emerging global pandemic. That February, I renounced my pastoral credentials with the Vineyard Churches of Canada. The move was in protest to their final and official position regarding same-sex relationships. The Vineyard opted to confirm a "traditional" definition of marriage. The wider implication was how LGBTQIA folks would belong in the denomination. In other words, they would not be permitted to live out their whole selves. Pastors were forbidden from performing same-sex marriages. The outcome was disappointing but not a surprise. It was a foregone conclusion despite a performative six-month decision-making process. My resignation wasn't a surprise either. I was one of a handful of pastors nationwide, and the churches with those pastors, who opted to leave the denomination. Usually, this kind of breakup is big news. But since the Vineyard in Canada is small, and the pastors leaving relatively insignificant (at least in terms of the size of their tithes), the breakup dissipated like a deep exhale into a frigid Canadian winter's eve.

As a cisgender man I'm not a gender minority. However, I am multiethnic and a person of color. My existence in my skin means something in virtually every single Protestant denomination in the West (Catholic too, I'm sure, but I can't speak for them). With rare exception, you won't see someone like me in a senior role in the church or denomination apart from ethnic communities. The rule, based on design and tradition, is that white men are the key leaders. That sounds like a generalization until you do an historical survey of church leadership in your denomination. In fact, the vast majority of Christianity in the West has been exclusively built and led by white men. There are some changes today, but they seem to be the exceptions to this unwritten rule. Why this persists deserves interrogation and dismantling, which we will do in chapter 6.

Giving up my license was performative and my rationale to leave simple (to me at least). How the Vineyard approached marginalized people like those in the LGBTQIA community previewed how the institution would face deeper wounds like institutional racism. Sexuality and race are two separate issues, but they are also related. Both represent marginalized groups faced with the same impediment—white supremacy. Preserving power for the existing power holders, and their dominant way of thinking and being, is an underlying purpose of institutions. Institutions are not designed to change; they're fundamentally designed to keep things the same, a posture that comes at the cost of further marginalizing those who have faced abuse and seek justice. A small but powerful list of failures coupled with theological matters designed to exclude includes:

- Psychological or sexual abuse by church leaders
- White supremacy
- Same-gender marriage
- Christian patriarchy
- Syncretism with nationalism, militarism, or capitalism
- Theological issues of biblical literalism, hell, justice, suffering, evil
- A posture of fear about the end of the world, pluralism, atheism, critical race theory
- A stance of being anti-science, anti-climate change, or anti-vax

This is only a short list of immutable postures churches adopt that cause internal dissonance or direct harm. To add insult to injury, many parishioners have become accustomed to church leaders protecting the institution at all costs when allegations of harm emerge. Even if it comes at the expense of victims and those seeking ardent reform and ultimate justice. The Roman Catholic Church's continued debacle surrounding residential school reparations, as well as clergy sex abuse scandals, comes to mind. The current conduct by the Southern Baptist Convention in its inability to faithfully respond to widespread clergy abuse accusations is another recent example.

Walking away from it all may be the healthiest alternative, at least temporarily. When church community detracts from your pursuit of wholeness, and ultimately your health, it's time to go. The negative experiences take a toll, and when harm accumulates, eventually the cost to stay outweighs the cost to leave. That always means some varying degree of loss. Nonetheless, exit is necessary to survive and does not require permission. We shouldn't have to assimilate to dominant cultural expectations or put our bodies on the line in order to taste a modicum of belonging.

When we look at these four options of church belonging, none of them seem suitable. Each one seems to perpetuate some hinderance to belonging. Does this mean leaving is the only viable choice? Or is there a more beautiful way where we, and people like us, can fully belong? When we read and observe the picture that Jesus had in mind, we notice tantalizing clues of a better way. Christ's ministry sought to break down dividing walls, subverting common perceptions of belonging in favor of an expansive scope of kingdom inclusivity. This is why I find it odd that churches are not more attentive to ensuring that all people can belong and flourish. It's the way of Jesus! A faith of radical inclusivity rooted in the Jesus worth reclaiming. To do so we will need two things. We need to go deeper to expose and name the root foundations that are inhibiting belonging, and we need a way to determine which pieces of Christianity are worth reclaiming. These are scary questions, but through this unknown wilderness our ultimate liberation is found.

# PART II

# DECONSTRUCTION

# 4

# The Woke Island

**PICTURE A LAKE** so vast that boats slip over its horizon and disappear. There are no clouds in the sky, only a faint haze matching the thick humid air. We are slowly churning through muddy waters in an old cabin boat chartered for the trip. It sports wooden benches for seating and a flimsy deck canopy barely hindering the piercing midday sun. Just as the temperature becomes too hot, and the rolling waves unbearable, a dot appears in the distance. As we approach it grows into a small island. The motor cuts out to signal we are crossing a threshold back into time. On cue, near the shore, tiny reed boats emerge, manned by single fishermen. They look like anachronisms straight out of Isaiah 18. But it's not they who are out of place—it's us. A boatload of Westerners ready to tour our island destination.

We disembark and begin plodding our way up a path of ancient paver stones lined by coffee trees and tropical shrubs. The path winds higher until we reach a clearing where, at the top of the island, sits an unusual monastery. The circular structure resembles a giant gazebo sitting in a clearing surrounded by mature sycamore trees. Despite the inaccessible location it's evident that here, on an island in the middle of a vast lake, sits a proud monument of history and worship. Pilgrims have visited this space for over 250 years. But it's not its unusual location that sets this place apart, it's what's *inside* that stops us in our tracks.

As we enter the main threshold it takes a second to adjust. The eyes are seeing things the mind is having trouble comprehending. Everything seems familiar yet out of place. This structure holds an outer round court, an inner court, and a square structure in the middle called the holy of holies. Lining the walls is continuous biblical iconography painted in vibrant reds and blues in ways I have never seen before. I can't decipher the stories entirely, because there are no words, only vaguely recognizable pictures. I think that's Mary, mother of Jesus. I think that's the Trinity, but I've never seen them depicted like that. The art is beautiful yet simultaneously out of place. In the middle of nowhere, away from my Western eyes, sits a visual marvel in one of the poorest countries on the planet. The thought crosses my mind: This shouldn't belong here. But then I realize the audacity of the claim. After all, the only thing out of place on the island with the unusual monastery are the tourists.

## ETHIOPIA

In the spring of 2008, I ended my seminary studies by participating in a travel study program. Our journey sought to discover, or rather rediscover, ancient forms of Christianity beyond Western familiarities. We ended in Israel having crossed into Jordan and Palestine prior. However, the start of our adventure began on Lake Tana, Ethiopia. Ethiopia boasts many beauties yet harbors outright desolation. It is one of the poorest nations in the world despite its rich history and natural resource potential. Lake Tana is the country's largest lake and is the source of the Blue Nile, which if legend proves true, flowed through the garden of Eden too. It's not the only claim in the region. The unusual island monastery is one of hundreds dotting the country. In the northern city of Lalibela, there's a UNESCO heritage site covering Ethiopia's rock-hewn churches built in medieval times. Legend has it angels descended from heaven to construct the last one—the Church of Saint George—in one evening. It remains standing at over one hundred feet *down* into volcanic rock.

Ethiopia's fame doesn't end there. These lands and people are mentioned specifically in the Bible forty-five times. The Ethiopian eunuch in Acts 8 undergoes a momentous conversion experience. Perhaps the reason he was even venturing to Jerusalem to begin with is rooted in the most famous appearance: the Queen of Sheba and her visit to King Solomon. The story in 1 Kings 10 is expanded in the national epic the *Kebra Nagast* with additional details. In it, Queen Sheba returns home pregnant, bearing a son named Menelik. He eventually returns to Jerusalem to meet his father, and despite pleadings to stay, returns home, although not empty-handed. Culture and relics were brought from Israel, where some were eventually assimilated.

Today, Ethiopia retains a lasting legacy of ancient Judaism that's combined with Orthodox Christianity. Ethiopians still practice some of the oldest forms of Jewish (now Christian) worship in the world. The same instruments, the same liturgies, even replica tablets and arks are paraded around church buildings. But perhaps the most extraordinary claim by Ethiopians, one most Westerners would only associate with Indiana Jones, surrounds the ark of the covenant. Not a replica ark, but the *actual* one. I've seen the monastery it sits in, guarded by two monks with rifles. You can't go in to view it anymore, but it's there. Rumor has it, up until the mid-1980s, the ark made public appearances for special ceremonies. Ethiopia's distinction as one of the only two (or three if you count Eritrea) African countries that have never been colonized (although the Portuguese tried and the Italians had a recent go) is sometimes attributed to the power of the ark.

Immediately after the story of the Ethiopian eunuch, we encounter Saul's conversion. On the road to Damascus, Jesus confronts him, leading to the beginning of his physical and spiritual rebirth. His sight returns when something like scales fall from his eyes; new vision to see the world in different ways. My trip to Ethiopia was one of now many moments where scales have fallen from my eyes, waking to a deeper understanding about faith and belonging.

Between the tales are other notable historical moments. Northern Ethiopia was home to the Aksumite kingdom, which was second in the world to Christianize, just after Armenia and just before Constantinople. The legacy prevails today with over thirty-six million members of the Ethiopian Orthodox Tewahedo Church. They even have their own pope (they call him the patriarch).

Then there's the ecumenical Council of Chalcedon in 451 CE. A split occurred when the Oriental Orthodox Churches (not to be confused with Eastern Orthodox traditions) separated over language disagreements about the Godhead and personhood of Christ. References to the incarnate Christ as "fully God and fully man" are directly influenced by the Chalcedon Creed. It's a normal descriptor in Protestant and Catholic traditions. However, it was rejected by the Oriental Orthodox Churches. They adhere to a doctrine of Christology called *monophysitism*: Christ's divine and human natures are not distinct but one. Ultimately, the differences wind up being an issue of semantics (depending on whom you ask), but it was nuanced enough that it led to the split. Why is this notable? Ethiopia is a rare place on earth where a living form of Christianity exists undeterred by Western influence. It's not a decolonized form of Christianity—it was never colonized to begin with. That's part of the beauty of Ethiopia, and beautiful things are good.

I wasn't thinking about colonization in 2008, at least not directly. Nonetheless, the vibrant island monastery walls challenged my theological assumptions. I remember one picture in particular, about the size of a car windshield, displaying three identical white-haired, brown-skinned men, side by side by side. The desert father figures were in fact the three persons of the Trinity. Icons of the Trinity are rare. Depictions of God the Father are rarer still. But icons with all three persons of the Trinity in identical form? My Christian lens automatically questioned this representation, categorizing it in the "might be wrong" column. This is trinitarian heresy, I thought. Something inside of me was suddenly alert to how routine the audacity of this thought process was.

\* \* \*

Too often we question the validity of weird moments in church community, chalking them up to isolated incidents and effectively gaslighting our own experiences. Individual encounters are hard to ignore, but they don't necessarily lead us to search for the deeper reason why barriers exist to begin with. Those answers are found when we dare look behind the veil of church doctrine and tradition. To make sense of what we see we must also develop new awareness that can spot any malformed realities producing fundamental inequities. We need to develop new alertness to describe *what* is causing all that ain't right in the world. I believe the roots are white supremacy and patriarchy, and we have to work our way down to this foundation before building a renewed reality.

## WOKE

Sociologist, historian, and author W. E. B. Du Bois wrote about the idea of a double consciousness to describe the African American experience at the turn of the twentieth century. Today his work could also be generally applied to any visible minority. Double consciousness is "the sense of always looking at one's self through the eyes of others, of measuring one's soul by the tape of a world that looks on in amused contempt and pity."[1] Who are the "others"? It's those with cultural power, so in this case white folks. What is this "other world"? The dominant gaze produced by white culture and then applied to confine persons on the margins.

The colloquial term emanating from Du Bois, and other writers and thinkers, on self-consciousness is called *wokeness*. This term has regained popularity as movements for Black lives gain momentum. Generated organically at the time of the civil rights movement when Black thought leaders gained greater prominence, wokeness can be loosely described as the collective awareness that Black culture develops to recognize and name systemic violence on Black bodies. This is in stark contrast to the way contemporary white conservatives steal the term, in an attempt to both malign and dilute in one stroke, because of an engrained fear of losing a particular (white) way of life (which is also ultimately a fear of Black people and a belief in the illegitimacy of Black thought).

Today, staying or becoming woke has been co-opted by various movements as it has entered the modern lexicon beyond African American culture, yet it still holds a base idea of becoming self-aware of dominant systems and paradigms designed to subjugate people on the margins. At the heart of wokeness is the ongoing confrontation between Blackness and white supremacy. But white supremacy subjugates every marginalized body. Black folks may be racialized to the bottom of a color scale, yet all minorities must adhere to the terms and conditions of whiteness. Token exceptions who dutifully maintain the vestiges of white supremacy may be temporarily excluded, but eventually those on the margins must realize how belonging is reserved for the "ideal" body sitting at the top of the social ladder. No others need apply.

Terms and descriptions iterate over time; nonetheless we must be mindful not to appropriate words and their meanings from the intended audience. *Awareness* and *alertness* are appropriate alternatives describing how everyone can develop new consciousness regarding systems and beliefs built to suppress marginalized people from achieving the fullness of our humanity. This demonstrates that the fear white conservatives have over the word *wokeness* is misplaced (and is evidence the issue is not about what the word means, but who is saying it). Many Christian traditions fundamentally aspire for an individual revelation and recognition of personal sin. It's the theological implication of becoming alert to the ways that systemic sin impacts all things and all people. (More on this in chapter 6.) When we become alert to our sin, we can strive to adopt a new way in Jesus to upend its consequence. That means, even those at the top of the sociological food chain—white men—understand what it means to be aware of the systems that destroy.

The applications to our world beyond the spiritual and physical dimension of sin should be obvious from here. Christians understand how systems can ensnare; what matters is how we respond and work to subvert and upend those systems.

It's the child brought up to believe racism is an issue of the past and who then watches the real-time upheaval against Black, Indigenous, or Asian bodies. This dissonance forces a rethink: the passive assumption that we live in a post-racialized world is untrue.

Pastor Eric Mason takes the concept of wokeness and locates a response from within the church in his book *Woke Church*. It's one thing to be conscious of oneself and how oppressive systems are designed to subjugate people on the margins. Mason calls for another level of consciousness: *Christ consciousness*.[2] Christ consciousness adds "depth and character" to wokeness, and acts as a source from which to build a suitable response once the proverbial scales fall from the eyes. Therein lies a crucial feature as we develop vision to name items behind the veil inhibiting belonging: *responding* to systemic wrongs is required. It's one thing to become alert to the malformed foundations of institutional Christianity; it's quite another to work collectively for the righting of these wrongs. But let's acknowledge that's a leap. From new awareness about an old problem to an eventual solution is work that extends over a lifetime.

When we become alert to all that ain't right in the world and the church, we need to make sense of the impediments before moving forward. Before we engage the possibilities for liberation, that dream for better in the midst of brokenness, we have to face a confrontation first.

## CONFRONTING THE GAZE

During my time in Ethiopia I saw God at work beyond my Western comprehension. This disruption framed a new level of consciousness. I could not ignore God revealed to be much bigger than the constraints of my limited worldview.

Remember, church tradition in Ethiopia is older than the version Constantine legitimized in Rome.[3] As my paradigm shifted, a much larger question brewed. Where did the idea I could question the orthodoxy of Ethiopian church icons come from? The answer didn't take long to pinpoint. It was my religious formation in white evangelicalism that constrained my beliefs and understanding of the global body of Christ. It also produced a level of contempt in which the (white) evangelical understanding of the world was right, and all others inferior (most denominations have this posture). That needed to change.

How I'm shaped to believe is distinctly rooted in white European, and later white American, thought. Since Chalcedon, Roman Catholicism and Protestantism have had 1,550 years of formation during which they assumed authority to shape Christianity globally, particularly in the West. How I comprehend scriptures, understand theology, or picture God is filtered through this monolith of interpretation. Yes, there are nuances, but the nexus of trust and "truth" remains entrenched in white European thought. Just do a historical survey of your tradition to see whose voice has dominated since inception. Indigenous, African, South American input was either wiped out or deemed too inferior to contribute to the whole (or only considered good enough to inform ethnic groups but not white Christian traditions).

White exclusivity isn't necessarily evil, but it is woefully incomplete to develop an understanding of what it means to be Christian in a modern world. Most often the understanding is how to uphold a particular worldview, and one that doesn't seek liberation or belonging for all people. These traditions have produced and legitimized disturbing actions of domination, violence, colonization, abuse, and division, to name a few. That should lead us to confront a Christianity condoning these activities and ask, "Which traditions cause (or caused) harm, and which ones produce life?" That question stretches beyond religious thought. Whose gaze determines what's right extends into every cultural pipeline. Have you interrogated whose gaze gets to determine common norms pertaining to health, wholeness, beauty, spirituality, and virtually everything we share that makes us human?

Questions are good. They lead us to become alert to the way we have been shaped and formed to believe, eventually revealing the hidden systems that influence what is right and wrong. These are the same components inhibiting inclusivity and wholeness. Ask enough questions and eventually your journey will reach the bedrock of belief systems. Here, new questions emerge that challenge foundations, questions like, Can the Bible can be trusted? And whose interpretation of the Bible have I adopted? That inevitably leads us to a more chilling realization about Jesus—Whose Jesus have I been shaped to believe and accept?

Becoming alert to the ways the church has influenced our beliefs, and how those beliefs are in fact barriers to belonging, leaves us at a crossroads. A crisis of faith develops as we struggle to make sense of traditions and doctrines once hidden behind the veil. We are left to consider: Should we stay, should we go, and how do we choose what to believe? The answers lie in a journey through deconstruction.

## ON DECONSTRUCTION

When something ain't right, it sparks a process to determine where the problems are coming from. The questions we ask mark a stage of discernment called deconstruction. Our interrogation can be short lived, fitting for small matters of theology, or they can take on a full-blown dismantling of your Christian faith. For the latter, this level of scrutiny challenges the structures behind "why we believe," and ultimately "why did I believe it?" Since the catalyst to deconstruction is either a harm or something we deem incongruent with the way of Jesus, we do not require any permission to deconstruct. Rather, it's inescapable work for those searching for better.

I never asked permission to do the work of deconstruction, nor did I need it. In fact, my journey through deconstruction didn't start with that label. Growing up in evangelicalism, and later attending an evangelical seminary, I certainly clashed with key pillars like patriarchy, biblical literalism, rugged individualism, purity culture, and so on. But initially I tried to attribute all the weird in the churches as a fundamental problem of *mission*. Fix the theological understanding of mission and churches would fix the problem of belonging.

The popular approach while I was still ministering in evangelicalism was being "attractional"—a model of church that picked up steam in the late 1980s spearheaded by megachurches that found success adopting certain market-driven approaches to spur growth. (That very same approach solidified racial segregation.) Churches of all sizes tried to adopt similar principles. The result produced a contemporary church for "consumer Christians"—individuals who chose (and stayed at) a church because of the quality of music and preaching and internal programming. This approach had wild success for the few churches that could afford it, which came at the expense of all those who tried but couldn't. Ultimately, the largest churches grew not because they enhanced belonging, but because they had the biggest budgets to offer the best services to attract both lapsed Christians and Christians transferring from smaller, less resourced churches.[4]

The reactionary movement to the attractional church is the missional church.[5] Rather than getting people into a church service or building, the missional church ideal sought to incarnate Jesus in specific spaces like a neighborhood or network. In theory the posture is more relationally driven and mimics the early church in approach. But it, too, produces many of the same problems as attractional models. Namely, the movement is entirely dominated by white men. Deeper questions pertaining to neighborhood segregation, church segregation, racism, patriarchy, ecology, and other theological issues rarely warrant focus over the prime matter of discipleship. Ironically, discipleship is the vehicle to form Christians into new ways of believing and being. The trouble is, missional or attractional churches still have to contend with the same root problems of Christian and white supremacy. So a change in missiology won't sufficiently answer questions of belonging. It, too, must face the inquiry of deconstruction. For someone who never found belonging in white spaces and who has no ethnic tradition to rely on, my walk-through deconstruction began in earnest once my work in missional church planting hit a dead end.

## CONCERNS ON DECONSTRUCTION

*Seems like half of the [West] is questioning whether that religion they learned growing up is actually Christianity while the other half is telling them they might go to hell for even thinking about that.*
    —Bradly Mason[6]

A curious feature in American evangelicalism (which is different from Canada on this notable factor) is self-conferring the position of protector and gatekeeper to all Christian truth. This posture produces a certain response when theological or cultural presuppositions are challenged. When it comes to deconstruction, a slew of pastors, theologians, and other thought leaders are working hard to discredit the growing movement. There is an obvious disconnection between the chorus of voices restless for wholeness and the so-called "protectors" of religious orthodoxy whose bias is to preserve the institution. From inside the safe confines of the church walls, systemic problems are ignored at best, or hidden at worse. From inside, liberation for all people is not an objective—protecting power and tradition is. That includes conservative voices (who decry deconstruction as dangerous, bordering on anathema) and progressive ones too (who water down deconstruction to preserve the institution). Of course, having particular convictions is not a problem—every denomination has them—but assuming those convictions are absolutes that everyone must adhere to is.

Virtually all denominations have seen a decline in membership for well over a decade.[7] (Some mainline denominations have been declining unabated for sixty years.) This does not even begin to factor in the catastrophic losses of the global pandemic. Shouldn't church leaders, in our current reality, focus on the causes of decline rather than turning "deconstruction" into a pariah? Perhaps the simplest answer is the best one in this regard. Institutional Christianity has a vested interest in deconstruction because their own people (or the ones they have lost) are the ones deconstructing!

I often remark how the social media hashtags #exvangelical and #deconstruction (more so the former) are dominated by white thought leaders. I have an issue with this exclusivity but not with the demographic reality. White evangelicalism (and therefore white churchgoers) was a majority tradition in the United States.[8] It's no surprise that white Christians, or those who used to be Christian, are sharing their stories of encountering and confronting the various forms of abuse and toxicity. This is why we must question the motives of church leaders decrying deconstruction. There is more concern about the loss of inherited privilege in the day-to-day lives of Christian adherents than about addressing malformed roots. Ultimately, those questioning past faith experiences are rightfully processing all that detracted from the fullness of life, and are too busy tending wounds to pay attention to vain warnings from within.

I should note my view on deconstruction is biased as well, influenced by my journey and work in vocational ministry outside of institutional boundaries. For instance, I don't believe deconstruction means reformation. Reformation talk generally means preserving or merely shifting the institution. Deconstruction cares not about the preservation of power. Rather, it fundamentally interrogates the structures producing the power and inequality in the first place. That's not initially a call for destruction; rather, it's an understanding that liberation requires examining structural elements, then being prepared to cut away any infection.

Deconstruction dares to ask, in the pursuit of individual and collective wholeness, whether the institutional church is worth saving. If this process leads to the collapse of an institution, then that indicates there was little worth saving. The internal rot must have been so widespread that self-destruction was imminent. Ultimately, the fear of and concern with deconstruction emanating from inside the church hinders the discovery of malformed roots, producing harm that may not be redeemable. Therefore, there's no coordinated deconstruction effort bent on destroying churches or denominations. Rather, the growing number of individuals engaging in deconstruction indicates widespread internal problems. When more and more Christians begin to survey all that ain't right in their faith, obvious conclusions are made. Among them is to simply leave, and when enough pews are emptied, the entity starves. Deconstructing out of faith and community (like option 4 as described in the previous chapter) becomes the decision caused by harms worth escaping.

This is not to say deconstruction leads to de-conversion or renouncing faith. In fact, I champion the opposite. My work in deconstruction has resulted in a way *back*. Not back into the institution (although it could happen), but rather back to Jesus. Not white Jesus created in America or Europe, but the multiethnic brown Middle Eastern man who is God and who unceasingly stood with the marginalized because he, too, was on the margins. The Jesus who deconstructed culture and religion every time he proclaimed, "you've heard what was said," and followed it up with, "but I say to you. . . ." That's who we seek to reclaim, as the subtitle of this book suggests.

I believe reclamation is worth it and that this work offers more possibilities for future wholeness than leaving it all behind. The fear is realizing you're deconstructing alone in uncharted territory. But the feeling doesn't have to last long. Take your time to find your bearings, and when you do, turn your head up and find out you're not alone at all. There are countless people in communities around the globe asking the very same questions you are, and it is good. Of course, that doesn't mean I don't hear friends, or people online, hitting a wall in their journey and exclaiming, "I'm done with Christianity!" But I want to call back and say, There's still hope out there! If there were good pieces in our faith worth reclaiming, would you be interested in the possibility? With this in mind, here is my invitation into the grey space of deconstruction and the possibilities to reclaim new life.

## ONE INVITATION INTO DECONSTRUCTION

Without creating an absolute, I offer this starting definition in the bid toward reclamation: *Deconstruction is a pathway that may liberate us from all that seeks to make us less whole.* It involves questioning the foundations, beliefs, and formation of our entire faith.[9] As we develop our awareness about the barriers to belonging, and our collective pursuit for ultimate wholeness, deconstruction involves the work to

reclaim what gives life;
discard what does not; and
create beautiful tales.

These three components are meant to be broad enough to engage institutional-sized barriers while simultaneously small enough to engage what's going on in your own heart and soul. Both take time. Deconstruction is not something that can be rushed (unless you're rushing right out). A lifetime of Christian formation may take equally long to undo and rebuild into something new. It's a journey that often feels disjointed—like visiting the mystical island monastery in Ethiopia. Being exposed to a new expansive reality of God felt disorienting.

Your story defines your deconstruction. It may include experiences that are right in front of you, or ones that emerge later on as hidden traumas emerge at the most unusual times. They may be spurred by the story of a friend, or they may suddenly strike as you become alert to new layers of systemic inequalities. No topic is off limits, and as new layers come to the surface we can now ask, Do we discard it, do we reclaim and keep it, and how may we build into a more beautiful way that liberates us from all that ain't right?

# 5

# Naming the Powers

**CAN YOU SPOT** the meaning in the following number set? 104, 35, 38, 182, 751, 160, 161, 80, 73, 74, 15, 42, 84, 54, 215. How about 3,200? Anything yet? Although they look random, these numbers are connected. Each figure represents the confirmed body count of Indigenous children found buried near the grounds of former residential schools in Canada in 2021.[1] New technology has pinpointed forgotten or unmarked burial sites, increasing the previously reported totals in the National Truth and Reconciliation Commission report published in 2015.[2] The difference in 2021 was the collective national outrage as unfathomable numbers proved the original commission estimate of 3,200 a gross underestimate.[3] (Just as with the COVID-19 death count, during every round of edits I had to add to the figures.)

For 167 years, the Canadian government (the United States too) collaborated with eager church denominations to implement a mandatory assimilation program designed to extricate Indigenous children from their lands and teach them the ways of the white man. Displacing children from their families and communities was done to prevent escape and yield maximum cultural change. But the goal of assimilation never happened.

Instead, generational damage was inflicted. That didn't stop government policy from reflecting fundamental ideas white Europeans held against Indigenous people. Not only were Indigenous communities thought to be incompetent at raising their own children, but they weren't considered human enough to be permitted full inclusion into Canadian society. The only pathway was enfranchisement, which meant giving up Indigenous identity—of land and people—and adopting a European lifestyle. The lasting effects of the monumental residential school failure, along with other assimilation attempts like the Sixties Scoop, day homes, and the present day foster care system, amount to cultural genocide[4] perpetrated by state and church. And before you think these evils are from the distant past, the last residential school closed in 1996, well within the lifetime of most readers. The survivors absorbed the lasting impact of generational trauma that still marks every Indigenous family and community to this day.

## PREREQUISITE TO DECONSTRUCTION: NAMING

Deconstruction will send you repeatedly back behind the veil to search and identify all the malformed powers producing barriers to belonging. These barriers are not all exclusive to the church, but rather represent all-encompassing foundations of society. Systems like patriarchy and capitalism that shape how we function and the ways we view one another. Yet further down, there's another layer looming: bedrock. At bedrock lies *white supremacy*. The many isms like sexism, classism, militarism, ageism, ableism, racism, grow out of white superiority. You might be thinking, "But, Rohadi, white supremacy isn't the totality of all the powers and principalities, both seen and unseen, opposing the reign of God in our world!" Perhaps it's not the totality, but in our context white supremacy is the primary tangible system of domination that we need liberation from. We will place our focus here, teasing out the layers of white supremacy and how it acts as a foundational barrier.

Of note, every intersection mentioned, and every one that is not, exists within unique spectrums. I argue that white supremacy (with a side of patriarchy) affects them all. We understand that skin color (race) is the primary distinction in white supremacy, but the racial project extends into everything. For instance, heteronormativity and gender constructs are products of white supremacy. I'm not suggesting that intersections are experienced in the same way. As an able-bodied neurotypical cisgender man, I can only speak to my own privileged experience. For me, white supremacy is the primary barrier in my life. This root structure impedes wholeness, and exposing it will help us identify what goes in the discard pile. By naming white supremacy we can identify what we're deconstructing from and thereby decrease the risk of replicating the very harms that struck us in the first place.

## DEFINITIONS

*White supremacy* is the belief that whiteness and those classified as white are superior to people of all other categorized races. It is designed to create and preserve power and privilege in society. That doesn't mean white people are white supremac*ists* by default. But it does mean everyone is shaped and formed by white supremacy's cultural and structural force. White people are the prime benefactors of white supremacy, automatic recipients of its systemic advantages. That's a troublesome idea for many white folks to become aware of and accept. Individualism celebrates the "self-made man," and receiving "something for nothing" is looked down upon. Yet if you are classified as white, there is nothing you can do to avoid the benefits of whiteness, because they are bestowed. Pointing out these disparities can be difficult. The colloquial term to explain agitation when subjects of racism are brought to the forefront is called *white fragility*.

Many find it difficult to hear the words "white supremacy" uttered in public. Some even consider use of the term to be "divisive," citing the myth that we live in an age of racial progress. This perception is of course distorted, a worldview that emerges from the lap of privilege or ignorance. It supposes that racism doesn't exist so long as nobody utters a racist phrase. It's here where we as a society fall short. White supremacy is our foundation, most often operating out of view, and by not using its name we give it more power to linger unabated in the darkness. Without a name we will struggle to locate future liberation and wholeness. Plus, when it comes to the work of reclamation, if you're not dealing with white supremacy, are you even deconstructing?

Race is a social construct that defines caste and subsequent privileges. The language surrounding systemic racism is entering our modern lexicon, but we still struggle to capture the magnitude of supremacy. One useful alternative is to think of the race-based system as a *caste* system. Isabel Wilkerson writes this in her book *Caste: The Origins of Our Discontents*:

> A caste system is an artificial construction, a fixed and embedded ranking of human value that sets the presumed supremacy of one group against the presumed inferiority of other groups on the basis of ancestry and often immutable traits, traits that would be neutral in the abstract but are ascribed life-and-death meaning in the hierarchy favoring the dominant caste whose forebears designed it.[5]

When whiteness is superior, all other categorized races are beneath, with Indigenous and then Black bodies at the bottom.

Racialized prejudice—holding preconceived opinions about someone based on the color of their skin—plus systemic power equals racism. A simple formula to understand racism is this: *racism = power + prejudice*.[6] Anybody can hold prejudices like bigotry (discrimination of the other), xenophobia (fear of foreigners), homophobia (hate against queer folks), to name a few. But on its own, prejudice is not racism. The required element is *power*. Power is why claims of reverse racism fall flat. Without power in systemic and cultural forms, there is no racism.

What do I mean by power? I will adopt the common understanding of power as predominantly material. Power includes aspects of wealth, political or religious authority, and social influence. That links closely to the temptations of Christ and the three pillars of power interpreted by Jacques Ellul: economic, political, and ideological-religious.[7] As we also engage in the reclamation of Christianity, there is a realm of power beyond the material—the spiritual. In what manner spiritual aspects of power work is a matter of theological debate. I will engage theologian Walter Wink and his idea that "the Powers are both heavenly and earthly, divine and human, spiritual and political, invisible and structural."[8] He proposes, "The spiritual and physical aspects of the powers [are] inseparable but distinguishable components of a single phenomenon—power in its concretions in this world."[9] That's curious because just as belonging cannot be separated between individual and communal, neither can powers be separated between spiritual and material.

Power is also tangibly related to our everyday lives, affecting "how people relate to one another, and who is advantaged or disadvantaged within social interactions."[10] Note: Power is not inherently evil (Colossians 1:16). It can advance the Spirit of truth and the new reality for belonging that God has in store. Therefore, it's how power is, or is not, wielded and what purpose it serves that matters. Rev. Dr. Martin Luther King Jr., in his presidential address to the Southern Christian Leadership Conference, noted, "Now, power properly understood is nothing but the ability to achieve purpose. It is the strength required to bring about social, political, or economic change. Power at its best is love implementing the demands of justice, and justice at its best is love correcting everything that stands against love."[11]

The allure of power, the various provisions required to keep it, and the manifestations when power takes on anti-kingdom goals explains much of the *why* behind systems of evil. Why does it seek to perpetuate dominating forces undermining marginalized bodies? Namely, why does white supremacy exist in the first place, and how deep do its roots go? Although I'm not trying to provide a work of history, generating a connective narrative outlining some of the key monuments of white supremacist formation will help frame the magnitude of this hidden system.

My friend and musician Drew Brown and I once had a conversation about our widespread experiences with racism. "It's in the water," he exclaimed. I retorted, "It's not in the water, it *is the water*." Racism, and the root of white supremacy, is far more expansive than we give it credit for. It's not an additive to culture; rather, it *is* our culture.

In the post–civil rights era, mainstream culture has gone to great lengths to claim that racism, at least on the surface, is unacceptable in public, and that when it does occur it's an aberration. However, the suggestion that white supremacy and racism may be reduced to individual bad actors implies that we ignore how such individuals are formed. It fits the compartmentalization bill. We tend to separate how things might be related to one another and in turn ignore the wider implications. Reducing racism to individual acts produces a solution that is individual as well. So long as the offender repents, racism is cured. That's how we get contrived replies of "I don't see color" and "I don't have a racist bone in my body." It falls short of a deeper repentance surrounding formation. We need to ask, What produces racist thinking in people? Why does it exist in the first place? And what do we need to change to dismantle it?

The recent uptick in white supremacist rhetoric and activity, such as the attack on the US Capitol as well as the freedom convoys, demonstrate there's nothing isolated about white supremacy at all. What was supposedly unacceptable in public is now tolerated; what was said to be isolated is now revealed to be widespread across nations. So racism never went anywhere; it was merely kept under wraps for a little while. That's why we must continue interrogating the ways white supremacy is intertwined in society and the church. We must ask questions like, Why did white evangelical support for the forty-fifth president of the United States remain unchanged throughout his term?[12] Why did reverberating calls for racialized justice and Black lives catalyze opposition in white conservative circles (in and out of the church) in a bid to preserve white superiority? To return to Jemar Tisby, "When faced with the choice between racism and equality, the [white] American church has tended to practice a complicit Christianity rather than a courageous Christianity. They chose comfort over constructive conflict and in so doing created and maintained a status quo of injustice."[13] This confirms my retort—racism is the water, and it's feeding poison to the entire social ecosystem.

Will we succumb? Or is a greater hope at play? As white supremacy rears its ugliness, more and more bodies, marginalized or not, stand in its way. When we look at contemporary shifts in our culture stemming from the advent of the 2016 US election, and later the chorus of calls for justice in spring 2020, change is not only coming, it is here. It's no longer taboo to talk about racism—it's of critical importance to reconsider how our neighborhoods and cities deal with systems rooted in the past, and how all may experience belonging in the present. Even churches that used to be abnormally silent in the face of calls for justice are addressing their own failures as local congregations demand action.

## WIDER SPECTRUM

It's necessary to understand racism and the impact of white supremacy through a wider lens. I use these three terms to help with explanations: *endemic, systemic,* and *systematic.* *Endemic* means racism is everywhere in our context and persists in everything (the water). It's not restricted to individual expressions; rather, it's the exact opposite because nothing escapes the clutches of this power. *Systemic* describes the ways racist ideology and policy are built into the DNA of our institutions and culture, past, present, and future. *Systemic racism* is a term you have likely heard before that describes the fabric of nearly every colonial nation. History has not directly used that term until recently, but we will soon find out it's been here the whole time.

*Systematic* describes the intentional design—how systems (or castes) are built to ensure cultures are shaped to uphold white supremacy, how that culture in turn shapes individuals to believe and perceive, and then how individuals keep the whole cycle churning. What does this look like in action? Professor Chanequa Walker-Barnes outlines four pillars of how white supremacy works particularly when it encounters non-white peoples. The pillars, expressed in questions, are should we exploit them (*commodification*)?; should we eradicate them (*extermination*)?; should we vilify them (*demonization*)?; and should we assimilate them (*indoctrination*)?[14]

When did this cycle first begin and in what specific ways does it impact people? At this point we need to take a brief pause. I struggled with this question for the book. On one hand, if you're on the path toward belonging and ultimate liberation, you have to contend with and dismantle white supremacy. That requires exposing all its parts. On the other hand, white supremacy, from ideology to its perpetuating legacy of marginalization, is so vast it's daunting to even find a place to start. When one chooses a point then one must select which stories to tell. I think it's important, even for racialized minorities, to hear stories about different people groups. It's especially important for white folks see the impact of a system bestowing privilege. But one inevitably excludes through the untold stories, and in the process diminishes the magnitude of evil. I think about the voices I'm missing.

I thought about this and couldn't come up with a worthy solution that didn't read as disjointed or out of place at times. But perhaps that's part of it. Whiteness produces a disjointedness in all things because it is a foreign substance on the land— which is exactly where we find suitable orientation: the land. The land where our feet are literally touching now appeals to the stories it holds. The land doesn't forget. The land also doesn't measure time. Rather, its lasting memory absorbs all manner of history at once. We can also say (as a matter of theology) that God is not constrained by time either. God can see the power of white supremacy all at once, not only within a temporal sense, but as it relates to God's unfolding hope[15] for creation now and forever more. With this in mind, and noting that our focus will remain in North America, we return to the question. When did white supremacy first come into being, and in what ways does it impact people?

## DOCTRINES, MYTHS, AND REALITIES

If we turned the pages from 2022 all the way to the start, the opening chapter would land in the mid-fifteenth century. How do events from over 570 years ago affect us today? In every way. European power holders generated a powerful myth surrounding white skin superiority. This new understanding of order was used to develop and justify African enslavement specifically rooted in anti-Blackness. The nexus moment that legitimized both, and catalyzed European colonization, started with the formation of the Doctrine of Discovery.

You can't "discover" lands that are already occupied, but that's what Christopher Columbus tried to do. When early colonizers realized New India was in fact occupied, they already had an ace up their sleeves called *terra nullius*, Latin for "empty land." Author Sarah Augustine explains, "[*Terra nullius* was a] theological and legal doctrine that gave land title to Christian European states. . . . 'Discovered' lands were considered devoid of human beings if the original people who had lived there—defined as 'heathens, pagans, and infidels'—were not ruled by a Christian prince."[16] Plans of conquest were already in motion before Columbus. The understanding described what would happen with new land and new people: extract and exterminate. Permission to conquer, steal land, and eradicate people groups requires a violent and dysfunctional worldview. "The *terra nullius* doctrine became the cornerstone of the Doctrine of Discovery,"[17] a framework of legal and religious principles. Mark Charles and Soong-Chan Rah explain in their book, *Unsettling Truths*:

The doctrine emerged from a series of fifteenth-century papal bulls, which are official degrees by the pope. . . . On June 18, 1452, Pope Nicholas V issued the papal bull *Dum Diversas*, which initiated the first set of documents that would compose the Doctrine of Discovery. The official decree of the pope granted permission to King Alfonso V of Portugal "to invade, search out, capture, vanquish, and subdue all Saracens (Muslims) and pagans whatsoever, and other enemies of Christ wheresoever placed, and the king-doms, dukedoms, principalities, dominions, possessions, and all movable and immovable goods whatsoever held and possessed by them and to *reduce their persons to per-petual slavery* (emphasis ours) and to apply and appropri-ate to himself and his successors the kingdoms, dukedoms, counties, principalities, dominions, possessions, and goods, and to convert them to his and their use and profit."[18]

The connection can't be ignored. The Roman Catholic Church collaborated with the Portuguese Empire to vindi-cate European savagery. It permitted and justified "enslaving and seizing the land and possessions of anyone who was not a Christian, setting the stage for colonization as well as the enslavement of African people by Europeans."[19]

Land. There it is again. When your worldview is postured to understand land as a tool that needs to be subdued for the purpose of wealth extraction, it fundamentally harms the peo-ple on those lands. And that harm extends even further than the Indigenous people dispossessed from their primary means of survival and identity.

Fueling the New World conquest required a continuous supply of labor. Dispossessing African bodies from their indig-enous lands became the primary means to fill this need. Yet we must go even deeper to ascertain how the catastrophic Doctrine of Discovery captured everyone. White European colonizers displaced themselves from their lands as well. The culmination of extracting people not only had devastating consequences for marginalized bodies, but also catalyzed a new way to imagine identity. Without land as a contributing root source to identity, and already operating out of a malformed heretical idea, *whiteness* became the means to measure all people, "[a] way of organizing bodies by proximity to and approximation of white bodies. . . . Displacement worked together to enable a new ground for imagining identity. It is this new ground that enabled the formation of the racial self."[20]

Creating a worldview around exceptionalism also requires a form of dehumanization.[21] Although prejudice in various forms has existed since the dawn of time, white supremacy rooted in anti-Blackness is a modern construct that came fully into view after the formation of the Doctrine of Discovery. Slavery, as some try to emphasize, was not unique to the time. What makes the Atlantic slave trade stand alone was its sheer destructive scale and the way it legitimized itself to specifically enslave Black bodies (the commodification pillar). Enslavement became an exercise in anti-Blackness, bodies that were of less value because they were less human. That's what made this era distinct. The new caste system was created around skin color, with Black being the lowest tier. Systems, cultures, institutions were built on top of the expanding bedrock of white superiority, impacting all future iterations. That's what we inherit today.

The Atlantic slave trade operated with impunity for over four hundred years until America abolished slavery in 1863 (1833 if you were in the British colonies). The lasting and insidious effects on the descendants of enslaved Africans, and Black bodies in general, is however a present reality. For starters, as mentioned, many African Americans cannot trace their identity back to place or ethnicity. Both were lost as bodies were ripped from their indigenous lands to till indigenous lands not their own. How do you find total belonging if you don't know who your people are?

The crumbs from the table came in the form of emancipation: freedom without reparations. In America, the federal government briefly considered restitution after the Civil War. Freed people sought the fulfillment of a wartime order for "forty acres and a mule."[22] (Not that the government had the right to give away land that was never theirs to begin with.) The idea would have offered a means to survive. But the policy never materialized and any land that was given was mostly reclaimed by white landowners. It was, after all, the white man's mission from God to spread his dominion across the land, and expand he did. There's a name for this specific mission, too: Manifest Destiny.[23] The modern progression would be American exceptionalism, with a side of Christian nationalism. Both operating with undertones of white supremacist ideology and practice.

Myth-making along with supporting legislation combined to fuel conquest and wealth extraction while simultaneously legitimizing marginalization by defining cultural narratives as well. Manifest Destiny came on the heels of a made-in-America version of the Doctrine of Discovery, the landmark 1823 Supreme Court ruling *Johnson v. M'Intosh* that effectively legalized land theft from, and displacement of, Indigenous people. Manifest Destiny became a powerful American narrative used to validate settler colonialism and fuel expansion westward. That eventually culminated in the Mexican-American War, expanding US territory even further—by nearly one-third.

The Reconstruction era immediately after the American Civil War is another example. The struggle for newly freed

African Americans, and Indigenous people, was fraught with ongoing subjugation and demonization coupled with the barrage of policy shifts employed to entrench white power. Disenfranchisement of African Americans reached critical mass in the Southern states and significantly curtailed civil rights, ushering in the age of segregation. White Americans readily bought into the new Jim Crow era that separated all aspects of life: housing, jobs, education, healthcare, and church life. It was a hundred years after the end of slavery before the rise of the civil rights movement, a movement that challenged segregation and new narratives that after the Second World War, society had somehow managed to land in a post-race utopia.

I'm always surprised how many people today believe we exist in a post-racialized world and even try to invoke the voices of Rev. Dr. Martin Luther King Jr., Malcom X, Rosa Parks, W. E. B. Du Bois, and others in support. None of these leaders sought to appease the comfort of white moderates in the search for justice. Rather, all expressed vision for liberation, and most through nonviolent measures.[24] Their call was radical and remains so today because of how little has changed. Yes, some progress has been made, but the root system of white supremacy remains.

## CANADA TOO

The concept of land ownership transformed the Americas and, unsurprisingly, Canada as well. A relatively recent Supreme Court of Canada decision, *R. v. Sparrow (1990)*, references the US Supreme Court *M'Intosh* decision to emphasize, "There was from the onset never any doubt that sovereignty and legislative power, and indeed the underlying title, to such lands vested in the Crown."[25] Curiously, how North America regards the First Peoples and their land differs from the Royal

Proclamation issued in 1763 by the British Crown. Within the proclamation, Indigenous people retain land title until ceded, if ever, by treaty. There are some regions in Canada today where different Nations have signed treaties (I live on Treaty 7 territory). Whether those treaties came into existence through a fair process is a matter of debate. Whether the Royal Proclamation created positive relationships between settlers and Indigenous people is not. When Canada became a nation in 1867, the then British North American Act (antecedent to the Canadian Charter of Rights) included Section 91(24), which gave authority to the federal government to make laws regarding lands reserved for the Indians, and regarding the Indians themselves. Today, extensive legislation found in the Indian Act controls Indigenous life. Up until a revision in 1951, "the Indian Act defined a 'person' as 'an individual other than an Indian.' An Indigenous person's only avenue to being recognized as a 'person' was to give up their Indian status, which was known as voluntary enfranchisement."[26] Of note, Indigenous people were only granted the right to vote federally in Canada in 1960.

This chapter began with the story about unmarked graves at old residential school sites in Canada. The search is expanding around Canada and into the United States. The purpose of residential schools was defined in the *Report on Industrial Schools for Indians and Half-Breeds* written for the federal government. In it, the now infamous words summed up the ultimate efforts of the program: "Kill the Indian in the child." The vessel to propagate the colonial arm was the church, which eagerly collaborated with the federal government. The allure of denominational expansion coupled with missionary efforts to convert pagans (remember the Doctrine of Discovery) was a temptation too great to ignore. In the end, church-run residential schools were instruments of evil that destroyed cultural identity and inflicted generational traumas.

## BUT THAT WAS A LONG TIME AGO . . .

*Systemic. Endemic. Systematic.* I'm always dismayed but never surprised when the subject of racism evokes the oft cited phrase of "Well that was a long time ago, get over it." A total undermining of personal experience and systemic reality. It's a plausible retort in a society where, up until recently, talk surrounding race was (still is) taboo. Racists are bad apples who do not reflect the progress of the bunch. But the truth for people on the margins, and all people for that matter, is that white supremacy continues to *commodify, exterminate, demonize, and eradicate.*

White supremacy still confines Indigenous peoples to reservations. It still won't acknowledge land title, still won't ensure potable drinking water is available on all reserves.[27] White supremacy built a substantial loophole in the Thirteenth Amendment that keeps slavery legal in American penitentiaries. Lawmakers, judges, police, and prison owners then built a cycle to incarcerate Black and brown bodies at record pace.[28] White supremacy maintains a US legal system around the execution of unjust laws (war on drugs, anybody?)[29]—yet another avenue to systemically brutalize and denigrate based on skin color. White supremacy builds immigration policy that incarcerates migrants with irregular status, imprisoning men, women, and children in the same facilities that interned Japanese people. White supremacy readjusts the rules on a whim, invoking discriminatory practices on "foreign" faces like the Chinese. An immigration head tax (and various other taxes) was imposed on Chinese immigrants when western expansion needed cheap labor and slavery was no longer an option.

White supremacy places Asian bodies somewhere in the middle of Black and white, luring with promises of wealth in exchange for quiet assimilation. White supremacy reminds the quiet assimilators that we, too, must face the terms and conditions when assaults of "China virus" and "kung flu" occur. White supremacy vilifies entire people groups, their values and religions, when they don't match expectations of the dominant gaze, calling them terrorists or rapists. It ignores those faces when they till the produce fields, offering no suitable labor protection in the cycle of indentured servitude. Any of these ring a bell? It's not a long time ago. For some of us, this is our reality today.

## WHITENESS

"I can't be held responsible for things done in the past." That's often a line I hear from someone learning about the way systemic forces are still at work in the present. On one hand the defense makes sense. White folks today didn't write the Doctrine of Discovery. The vast majority do not shape present-day public policy either. Therefore, it's not so much the responsibility for failures of the past as it is for what is being done with the inheritance bestowed in the present. Let's end by clarifying what these privileges look like.

After unpacking the foundations of white supremacy, its widespread nature and purpose and the ways it functions in the past and present, we prepare to do the same for the cultural normative called *whiteness*. When we describe the demand to assimilate, whiteness is the "what" you are assimilating into. The question from chapter 4, about "whose gaze" determines the norm, was a reference not to a particular individual, but rather to the social construction that tries to represent the whole. Theologian Willie Jennings adds, "'Whiteness' does not refer to people of European descent but to a way of being in the world and seeing the world that forms cognitive and affective structures able to seduce people into its habitation and its meaning making."[30]

Remember, racism = *power* + prejudice. Whiteness is the system and the means to hoard the power. It is the "mortar holding together the fortress of white supremacy, and if it crumbles, those walls will inevitably collapse."[31] This fortress provides no escape and no option to deny its blessing and privileges once bestowed on an individual. The identity, apart from its power, lacks specific roots (such as land) and is often described not by what it is, but by what (or who) it is not. Whiteness also bears an inherent cost. Often it replaces ethnic identity. Power and inherited privileges, even when they come at the expense of Black and brown bodies, become the standard elements associated with what it means to be white. We're seeing this phenomenon play out in real time as the demographics in North America shift. White folks have a genuine concern. If the power associated with whiteness and a white majority erodes, white identity will go with it.

Who is white reflects the peculiar range of whiteness, and yet the requirements to be white, in the words of author and historian Vine Deloria, "are not very rigorous."[32] Because the primary goal of whiteness is power preservation, the boundaries of whiteness expand when necessary. What region and time you live in dictates whether or not you're considered white. At the turn of the previous century, Irish, Italians, and Ukrainians took turns as marginalized ethnic minorities. As time moved on, whiteness expanded to include minority groups that looked white. If you have a Ukrainian babusya or Italian nonna, they have stories about ethnic prejudice. Today, although ethnic roots may remain strong, new groups are added into whiteness so long as they adhere to the rules of anti-Blackness and power hoarding. The invitation to maintain the racialized status quo affords the opportunity to thrive under the advantages of whiteness.

Whiteness doesn't end with power. The proliferation of white supremacy has shaped almost every culture on the globe by rewriting standards to match the white gaze. Back to Jennings: "White self-sufficient masculinity is not first a person or a people; it is a way of organizing life with ideas and forming a persona that distorts identity and strangles the possibilities of dense life together."[33] Colorism is an example of how whiteness has shaped beauty. Lighter skin tone and rounder eye shape are seen as being more desirable, and the demand to assimilate fuels a billion-dollar beauty industry for skin lightening creams and plastic surgery.

In the West, terminology of "white passing" applies regardless of ethnicity. If you draw roots from the Arab Peninsula or Latin America or even as an Indigenous person, so long as you blend into dominant culture—if you look white—you can reap the benefits of whiteness. Just don't tell anyone about the quiet arrangement. (Other quiet arrangements include folks who don't "look" queer, or neurodiverse, or disabled.) Remember, the first measure we place on someone is the color of their skin. What you do with that information is the question. Black and brown people know we will never fit into whiteness, although temporary inclusion is permitted to uphold matters of anti-Blackness and anti-Indigeneity. That's how Asians fill the model minority myth with an "in between" existence, with white privilege on one side and Black or Indigenous vilification on the other. The rise of anti-Asian racism during the global pandemic was a stark reminder that we must adhere to the terms and conditions of white supremacy too.

## TERMS AND CONDITIONS

The last time I downloaded a new app I decided to read the fine print. Most companies have a basic set of terms and conditions that are around five thousand words. Some are much longer. Facebook has three different policies that you must agree to with one checkbox. The total number of words for all three is just over ten thousand. That's about a fifth the size of this book! Let's be real, unless it's a mortgage, we don't read the terms and conditions. We click "Yes" because it's the only way to participate and move forward.

Whiteness is like the terms and conditions we never read yet must approve for social participation. Click "Accept" and figure it out as you go. Even if we read the terms, we can't object. Want a house? Sign the terms. Want to make money for a house? Sign the terms. Don't like being discriminated against? Well, you didn't read the terms. Want to blend in? Read the terms, it's in the assimilation section. Even if you follow the terms and conditions to the letter, there's a clause saying new terms may be applied without notice just to remind people on the margins that a hidden system is at work. The choice appears to be a take-it-or-leave-it scenario. But here's the thing—another option is out there.

When we name the powers that seek to make bodies on the margins less whole, dragging those powers from behind the veil and into the light, we discover their essence is not absolute. Searching for belonging? Subvert the terms and conditions and opt for a more beautiful and inclusive way of being. In fact, every time we ignore the terms for better, we opt for resistance. Resistance to all that ain't right in our world in the search for true belonging.

# 6

# Discard the Church?

**WHEN MY SECOND CHURCH PLANT** launched we boasted a level of diversity in ethnicity, gender, and sexuality that I had personally never experienced before in a church community. As a multiethnic person, the environment was a gift to me. Imagine my disappointment when our leadership crew failed to handle the pillar of white supremacy with ease.

One Christmas, a younger Chinese woman on our leadership team shared a recent experience she had at the grocery store. An older white man wearing a Santa hat was browsing the frozen food aisle.

"Merry Christmas!" she said.

His retort was immediate. "You speak very good English, where are you from?"

For someone in her early twenties, this type of abrupt interaction was thankfully uncommon, albeit shocking. The visible minorities in our leadership group were shaking their heads. Some of the white people didn't think it was a big deal.

I decided to chime in. "That's white supremacy in action."

Using the term "white supremacy" often elicits discomfort in those who rarely hear it uttered. I didn't think it would be an issue in our leadership group. Our church was culturally entrenched in the arts and hip-hop community, after all. But I assumed very wrong. Some of our white team members were offended that I used such a strong term to describe what they saw as a routine interaction. They even tried to defend the man.

I explained the problem. "The older man is maintaining a worldview where whiteness is normative and Asian faces are foreigners who speak broken English. He's playing a role in determining who belongs on the land.

A team member felt that terms like *whiteness* and *white supremacy* were "divisive" and offered correction by quoting from the Bible. Galatians 3:28 to be precise. She said, "We are all equal before the Lord, there is no Jew nor Greek, slave nor free . . ."

At this point I realized the team was not on the same page. "Saying 'white supremacy' is not divisive," I countered. "It's giving name to the existing prejudice. With a name we can describe the powers marginalized folks encounter. The question is, What will we do as a team when someone shares an experience of being marginalized and othered? Will we empathize and sit in the discomfort?" As one of the pastors, I wanted to have a clear position that our church couldn't ignore systemic injustice. We had to confront it, *but* we would face the experience together. Sadly, three people left our church over the prospect we would take the work of racialized injustice seriously.

Diversity, like true belonging, must be cultivated. Without intent, churches can build diversity on the outside, but the structures inside remain steeped in cultural and theological whiteness (option 3 churches). Churches that question bedrock formation of cultural and theological whiteness invite internal conflict among the congregation (and often from beyond as well). I want to acknowledge that it's hard to see white supremacist formation in our own traditions, or more poignantly in ourselves.

This highlights the need to deeply interrogate Christian formation in order to spot the ways we have been malformed. Layers that have operated undetected for centuries.

## BACK TO SYSTEMS AND POWERS

"There is within Christianity a breathtakingly powerful way to imagine and enact the social, to imagine and enact connection and belonging."[1] These words are part of the introduction to Willie Jennings's book *Christian Imagination*. It's a line that also partially describes the pursuit of this book—the chase for an imagination that fully grasps connection and full belonging. But then we have impediments: "Christianity in the Western world lives and moves within a diseased social imagination."[2] When we interrogate the proliferation of cultural whiteness, and the ways it shapes every facet of our modern culture down to our spiritual being, we have to ask the same questions about the church. We have named the disease as white supremacy, the bedrock system of power that not only undermines belonging but represents a primary force opposing God's hope to redeem all things. This systemic evil is fully active within the church, where we're not merely culpable, but prime architects.

Many leaders scoff at the notion that systemic injustices like white supremacy and abuse exist. This is particularly difficult in traditions that assume a "protector of God's truth" posture. If systemic problems do in fact exist, acknowledging them would be an admission that fundamental belief systems and power structures are flawed. It's easier to undermine systemic claims and preserve the institution. But here's the reality: Christianity has no qualms with acknowledging systemic evil—it's called sin! Many systems of belief (systematic theology) assign a condition to humanity that's inexplicably inherited through the transgressions of one man. Adam curses all in a moment we call "the fall." The result: every human is now marked by this "original sin." It's essential theology for virtually every tradition. This means that understanding the power of systemic problems is a core competency in Christianity. The real issue is one of power preservation. It's why many churches undermine any attempt to interrogate past and present connections to white superiority and systemic racism. This despite the rising calls from the margins to dismantle these oppressive features.

There's another curious feature in the Bible surrounding the relationship between powers and systems. Theologian Walter Wink argues that the New Testament period held a wide understanding of systemic powers reflected in the Greek word for "world," *kosmos*.[3] We think of it today as the known universe, which is fine when appropriate. Depending on the context, however, the accurate translation is in fact *system*. This is the case in the epistle of 1 John, when the systems on earth attempt to upend God's hope for restoration. For if anyone loves the subjugating systems, the love of the Father is not in them (to play off 1 John 2:15b). Go ahead and have a look, and see how the teachings of Jesus and the writings in the New Testament gather new meaning.

So not only was the term *system* well understood by the early church and Jesus, but it neatly informs how we may confront systemic evil today. The next question we must ask is, How did systems of marginalization emerge from *within* the church? From Roman pontiff Nicholas V and his orchestration of the Doctrine of Discovery to the syncretism of white nationalism within white evangelicalism and fundamentalism today, and to everything spanning five centuries in between, the central problem remains malformed power. That wasn't always the case. The pursuit of cultural power would have been considered uncharacteristic for the church in its first three hundred years.

## CHURCH AS CRITIQUE

Early Christian community was designed to embody the teachings and character of Jesus. This produced a profound ethic of love that produced radically inclusive community. This church bore witness to the way of Jesus (Acts 1:8), including representing him in public too (2 Corinthians 5:20). Christians did not conform to the patterns of Caesar, they did the exact opposite (Acts 17:7). It was a posture that carried the constant threat of death and persecution. As the underground church grew, they assumed a natural, albeit perilous, position as primary critique to the Roman Empire. God's kingdom against Caesar's, and the two do not mix. This all changed about three hundred years after Jesus rose from the grave.

In the year 327 the Council of Constantinople convened with the who's who of church leadership. (As noted earlier, Constantinople was the third state to Christianize. The first was Armenia and the second was Axum in modern-day Ethiopia.) The primary topics of concern were a combination of the filioque controversy and modalism. The latter contributed trinitarian roots for the eventual confession called the Nicene Creed. (This creed is particularly important today as proponents of patriarchy, or the "traditional definition of biblical manhood and womanhood," reject the creedal confession and commit literal heresy by adopting a position that God the Son is subordinate to God the Father. Again, heresy.) Although the pursuit of institutional power was not a central purpose to the gatherings, it was the result, and it has shaped the church ever since.

A collaboration between church and empire had pragmatic benefits for the early Christians. The constant pressure of persecution abated. Security is not a bad thing, but it certainly changes the function of the church. No longer were they the primary critique to the empire; rather they became its muse. Becoming the state-sponsored religion of Rome also provided an inheritance of power. That initially formed the Roman Catholic Church, but virtually every major Christian expression from the eventual West emerged from this relationship and suffers from the effects of ill-gotten gains.

The chase for dominating power, and God's disdain for it, is a consistent theme throughout Scripture. It was the allure of total power that drew people to build the Tower of Babel. It was the clutch of power that compelled Pharaoh to harden his heart. The liberated ancient Hebrews eventually settled in a land, but if we're alert to the voice of the marginalized, the eventual development of Israel's power turned them into a colonizing nation rather than one building relationship with land and people. Prophet after prophet warned Israel about their meandering power pursuits at the expense of God's story, calling them to be people who chased justice until it flowed like a river, exhibiting a profound care for the marginalized and the poor, and all associated with God's unchanging hope to right every wrong.

What sustains godly power is justice and righteousness (Isaiah 9:7), not wicked decrees or harmful laws (Isaiah 10:2). Kings and kingdoms all passed away, culminating in the eventual exile (the conquering and captivity of Israel by the Babylonians) and the final destruction of the Jewish temple by Rome some thirty to forty years after the crucifixion of Jesus. Scripture is a cohesive narrative that tells a tale that God wants people to reflect something unique, and when we stray from this specific call there's a fracturing of relationship.

The allure to expand dominating power became the new filter for the church. Rather than "Blessed are those who wait on the God who loves justice" (Isaiah 30:18; 61:8), it became "Blessed are those who expand powers and privileges given by empire." When the church began to develop its relationship with the empire—with power—the DNA changed. No longer were the concerns about critiquing empire (and surviving); rather, it created accommodations to preserve it. The ideals and ethics shifted from a subversive church that welcomed all—including women—into community, embodied humility and love, and sought peacemaking and justice, to a church of conquest, violence, and Christian supremacy. The erosion from core principles shown by early Jesus followers moved the goalposts on what it meant to be Christian, paving the way for further deterioration to accommodate warped thinking.

The marriage between church and state altered the former's trajectory. The church quickly adopted patriarchy and virtually castigated the revolutionary inclusivity that had made it unique. Christianity went from margins to center as the Roman Catholic Church assumed command. Once it had established itself, plans of conquest soon followed. The Crusades were the early forays into expansion and preservation. These beginnings of Christian imperialism were also the precursor to Christian supremacy.

This was not a Roman or Roman Catholic phenomenon either. As Christianity spread northward into Europe, each kingdom sought ways to legitimize its power alongside church authority. The church for the most part moved in support. It was the Roman Catholic Church that generated and approved the Doctrine of Discovery. As described earlier, these malformed plans of conquest provided supposedly God-given authority for any kingdom seeking to uphold church doctrine. The church produced and affirmed anti-Blackness. The church built theological justification for slavery. It became a benefactor of the Atlantic slave trade. The church built new ontology labeling Black and Indigenous bodies as less human. The church tried to assimilate and annihilate Indigenous people and practices, deeming them pagan, savage, unworthy to contribute to the purity of European thought and process. The church legitimized segregation. The church adopted the "Protestant work ethic" to fuel western expansion and wealth accumulation. The storied relationship between church and empire produced and maintained white Christian superiority through violent domination and subjugation. All of this, and we haven't even hit the twentieth century.

## RELIGIOUS RIGHT IS WHITE

Like the early church who opposed empire, marginalized voices have long resisted Western churches steeped in cultural whiteness. Today, as demographics shift, communities on the margins are generating renewed strength. Demands for change are causing certain alarm in dominant traditions. You can hear it in the vain calls from conservative Christianity to preserve culture, be it nationalistic or religious. The fear of losing inherited privilege has steadied conservative focus to retain the last vestiges of power and privilege. This course of action is not particularly new. In fact, there's a cycle.

The emergence of the religious right in the United States (which has global impact, too) was spurred by the loss of a "particular way of life" on the heels of desegregation. Race was the primary motivator behind its formation. Private Christian universities fought federal legislation to retain segregation. The thought of interracial relationships was too much for the white psyche to bear.[4] Although the fight failed, the consolidation of religious conservative power was born. Using fear as a primary motivating factor, every future cycle of outrage was fueled by a new scapegoat. After targeting racialized minorities (specifically Black bodies), attention turned to vilify the LGBTQIA community (the "gay agenda"), and later immigrants and refugees. The guise to maintain momentum came under the narrative of preserving "family values." But as historian Kristin Kobes Du Mez tracks in *Jesus and John Wayne*, this value has been a colossal failure, producing traits of toxic masculinity, rampant abuse, and rugged individualism instead.

Although it is accurate to pinpoint white evangelicalism as the primary denominational vehicle bent on retaining racialized structures of white supremacy, they aren't alone. The most vocal and the largest, the Southern Baptist Convention, certainly fits the bill, especially because they specifically formed around protecting slaveholder religion. But they can't bear all the blame. Every white Protestant and Catholic tradition participates in upholding white supremacy from pew to parish. As Robert Jones writes, "White Christians and their institutions, especially at the local level, were not just passively complicit with but also broadly and actively resistant to claims of equality."[5]

## BAKED LIKE A CAKE

One of the simple joys during pandemic life has been watching television shows that require no mental investment. Comedy, cartoons, and cooking are my three Cs to television success. Two shows we began watching during the pandemic, and haven't stopped since, are *The Great Canadian Baking Show* and its British counterpart. I'm not a baker, but I do know once you put the wet and dry ingredients together and pop that batter in the oven, there's no hope the recipe can be changed. When chocolate goes in, carrot cake will never come out. The universal truth in baking: you can't change the flavor of a cake after it's been baked.[6]

Churches and denominations rooted in white hegemony are cakes baked with a recipe steeped in white supremacy. It's unavoidable formation, and no amount of fondant or sprinkles can change the flavor. You can only put the cake in the bin and start a new recipe from scratch.

The usual reply to the cake conundrum is "But not *all* cakes . . ." This sounds eerily familiar to the problem of "color-blind" racism discussed in chapter 5. If you can't see it, it must not exist. It's true that some denominations (or churches) lack an overtly racist history (say, condoning slavery or segregation or running residential schools), but they wrongly assume they are excluded from the bad cake mix. It's not a matter of if, but to what degree traditions are formed in white supremacy. Here's a quick recipe check to describe what I mean. Consider your past or present church or denomination and ask:

- Are churches racially segregated (or more specifically, monoethnic)?
- Who are the leaders? Who were/are the presidents, bishops, district superintendents, lead pastors, staff, or board directors?
- Are leadership positions dominated by white men?
- What ethnicity are historical leaders?
- Has the denomination been formed by diverse people, or is there only token representation?

- Is there diversity in the community? Or is everyone culturally the same?
- Are queer folks permitted full inclusion in community and leadership?
- Are women permitted to be lead pastors?

You may have noticed a theme of sameness in your answers. Maybe you already knew? Is it a problem when denominations or churches are exclusively formed through white male authority? Absolutely. At best it's incomplete, lacking distinct expertise to produce more inclusive ways to build community. At worst, white hegemony makes recognizing, let alone repenting from and repairing white supremacy, nearly impossible. Also at worst, the lack of diversity makes it difficult to recognize malformed ingredients that harm the margins. Failures of spiritual or sexual abuse, LGBTQIA exclusion, and rampant misogyny occur when organizational structures are designed to protect power holders over accountability. Harm in all its hidden and visible forms runs unchecked without leadership from the margins protecting community health and forming tools required for all to thrive.

As an aside, you may have considered an ethnic tradition in the questions above. These traditions are not devoid of toxic ingredients. All have to contend with malformed structures that seek to preserve power.

The cake conundrum raises an important question: Are any Christian traditions with American or European roots capable of producing a new way of thinking? To quote Joseph Drexler-Dreis, "Can theology, as a mode of critical reflection that employs core concepts and images with lineages grounded in the European experience, contribute to the task of decolonization?"[7] He argues aspects that can be reclaimed. I'm okay with

the assertion, but if it were such a real possibility, wouldn't it
have happened already? Ultimately, we still need a better way,
and it needs to come from a new source.

## WHAT DID MOSES LOOK LIKE?

When I lead a study on decolonizing Christianity, one of the first
questions I ask is, "What did Moses look like?" It may sound
like a bizarre question, but there is an interesting answer using
a little piece of information I picked up in the 1980s. Getting
a comic book insert every week at Sunday school was one of
the few incentives that got me to church service. You might
know what I'm referring to. Full-color four-page comics from
*The Picture Bible* were doled out to kids—for free. Everything
I know about the Bible today is rooted in these images. They
helped the stories come to life. Elijah carried up into heaven
on a full-page spread with bright red and orange flames con-
suming a chariot on fire being pulled by what were clearly
angel horses. Adam and Eve were two nude pinkish people
with luxurious yellow hair. The forbidden fruit, mmm, looked
delicious as it shimmered with a distinct fuchsia color and
Jell-O-like consistency. And Moses, well, Moses was ruggedly
handsome and had an uncanny resemblance to a middle-aged
Burt Reynolds. That's what Moses looked like—Burton Leon
Reynolds Jr.

Somehow my *Picture Bible* survived childhood, and I
recently had another look. With a few more years under my
belt I quickly realized the entire book lacks *a single character
of color*. Let me repeat myself so my point is crystal clear. The
entire *Picture Bible*, from Genesis to Revelation, does not con-
tain a *single* character depiction that isn't pink skinned. There
is, however, one anomaly. If you turn to the stories in Acts,
there is one figure way off in the distance. It's the story of the

Ethiopian eunuch. You know where this is going. Surely, the eunuch, from Ethiopia, is some kind of brown? Wrong. He's pink. No, the one anomaly is actually *the driver of the chariot* the eunuch is riding in (I know, that's not accurate at all). He's an off-grey, but I can't be sure if it's because he's so small the printer simply made an error.

Today, there are more illustrated book options that include Black and brown characters. Thirty years ago, these resources didn't exist. I had David with his piercing blue eyes and blond hair, Jesus with his piercing blue (sometimes brown) eyes and brown hair, and of course, Burt "Moses" Reynolds. *The Picture Bible* is a visual deception that formed my understanding of faith, and is only one example of how everything we absorb from Christian literature, theology, books, movies, sermons, songs all reflects the worldview and culture of its creators. Which is to say they all come with bias and presuppositions built in. Whether we are aware of how our faith is being formed by whiteness requires that level of alertness discussed in chapter 4.

## WHITE JESUS

You've seen the image before. Recently conditioned brown-haired, blue-eyed, California-style surfer Jesus with a slightly receding hairline posed in profile and staring longingly into the distance. The portrait painting was created during Jim Crow by an American commercial artist named Warner Sallaman. It is one of the most reprinted portraits of Jesus, and is displayed in many living rooms across the globe. Its popularity also dominates how Western Christians perceive Jesus and serves as a useful example of how whiteness defines Christianity.

Deconstruction asks not "Is Jesus real?" but rather "Whose interpretation of Jesus do you believe in?" Malformed theology must constantly adapt to regenerate a god made in a particular image. It produces a Jesus who acquiesces to the demands of powers like white supremacy. When you think of contemporary examples, the irony is palpable. Traditions espousing a white "warrior Jesus"[8] have actually created pushover Jesus. Jesus acquiesced to become the blond-haired, blue-eyed version who votes Republican, goes to church on Sunday, is a quintessential family man, has a Protestant work ethic, hates immigrants with irregular status, supports guns and war, spreads good old American democracy, and so on.

When we make Jesus look like someone in particular, we can turn around and claim that to be like this Jesus, you need to look that certain way too. Of course, it's easy to wag the finger at the most ridiculous examples of corrupted Jesus figures when we should be contending with the plank in our own eye. There are few church traditions and people who can escape the clutches and influences of white supremacy and whiteness. As we attempt to discern the "biblical Jesus," we have to come to a realization that there isn't one. That's not to say we can't reclaim a more credible Jesus, but we'll always speak our perspective into who that may be. Part of that is actually a good thing. The incarnation invites us to contextualize the stories of Jesus in our modern vernacular. We'll look more into this reality later.

For now, the challenge is to determine, Do we have the Jesus created from the seat of power. Or is it the Jesus that Mary sang about in her prophetic preview of a faith and community through the words of the Magnificat (Luke 1:46–55)? From her we garner a picture of what hope would usher in. The powerful are tumbled and the humble lifted up; the rich are sent away, and the hungry are filled; the proud are scattered while promised heirs are shown mercy.

Today we must search and embody Mary's song. A love so wide our churches no longer become storehouses of power, deceit, abuse, and white superiority. Should we stay within the safe confines of the church walls and do nothing? Do we just up and leave it all behind? Or do we find a few faithful and forgiving friends and imperfectly try to imagine a more beautiful faith with a breadth for a more beautiful embrace of belonging?

# PART III

# RECLAMATION

# 7

# Jesus for the Margins

**HERE WE ARE**—in the wilderness. Dear reader, I invite you into the possibilities of reclamation. In the wilderness one thing is certain: you don't need permission to discover your liberation. But where does one even begin? Discarding what does not give life might be easy, especially when you can name the source. But how does one determine what to reclaim without repeating the failures of the past?

Early in my first church plant I was helping a friend discern a big life change that would impact the whole family. The choices were stay in the city or chase a new job opportunity with the caveat that it would require relocating to another province. I wanted to help her make the "right" choice as we weighed the pros and cons. Putting on my pastor hat, I added the classic obligatory consideration to the mix.

"Between the two, which one do you think God is in?" I asked.

"I don't see it that way," she replied. "It's not a matter of which one will be better or worse, or which one God is leading us toward. I see it as, here are the two options, God is in both."

Her response struck me, and I've kept it with me ever since. God doesn't dwell in boxes, buildings, or cathedrals. God chases us, beckoning us to find our way into the fullness of who God made us out to be. Just as we named monuments to deconstruct, like white supremacy in past and present, so we can also identify signposts guiding us along a meandering pathway of reclamation. We won't find *the* pathway unto liberation, but we will find tools and vocabulary that can help illuminate a way out of obscurity.

This faithful pursuit, wherever it may take us, is one we do not take alone. Jesus is always with us. I know that sounds trite. There's plenty of past church trauma where (for me) evangelicals would chide other traditions, stating, "We're all about Jesus!" I mean I get it, and I do believe it to be true. But we're always looking through a filter that demands we ask, *Whose Jesus?* The domesticated caricature of white Jesus folding to the demands of his cultural masters? Or the brown multiethnic Jesus from the lands of ancient Palestine who was marginalized and centered the marginalized while announcing the inbreaking subversive kingdom of God? It's the latter, the incarnate Jesus who took on flesh—a body—to identify with our frailties and mark a path for renewal. We are now invited to participate in this new way of being, and the demands are that the last shall be first, and the first last.

Not only is there a renewed ethic to embody, but there is a mystical invitation too. As Jesus was crucified, the earth shook and the moon turned red. Down the road the temple veil tore in two, symbolizing the new relationship between God and humanity. Now our bodies become vessels—the new temple. A personal spiritual re-creation that transpires when the Spirit of God dwells within us. How does it work? Perhaps an invitation through a prayer, perhaps through a vision or a song. Our response follows the faithfulness of Jesus and embodies a specific relationship, through the Spirit of God, to be ultimately transformed in body, soul, spirit. This specific relationship is worth reclaiming. With it we must also include the vision for a new age to come within our world. One where the margins move to the center, the first become last, and the overflowing love that made the stars in the sky pours into all things. Where do we find such a story? You already know it in pieces. It's the story of God on a mission to rescue and redeem all of humanity, reconciling all things back to a place and space where all things are right. We need to make this connection, and to do so we'll go back to the beginning.

\* \* \*

*Once upon a time there was silence and the Creator.*

*A cataclysmic bang—or perhaps just a whisper—set the universe in motion, filling a vast emptiness with innumerable stars and planets. Within the cosmos sat a most peculiar grain of sand in the most peculiar spot. Earth. At first it sat formless and void until, like sections in an orchestra rising to their entrance, new creations appeared. The waters, the plants, the sun, and the moon. The birds of the sky, the animals on the land, the fish in the sea, and finally the bugs in your hand. Each one made with distinct purpose in the new garden, affirmed good and beautiful. But one more piece was yet to emerge.*

*One day, the Creator made humanity unique from all the rest. Image bearers—reflections of Creator's own image. An uncanny likeness in character, disposition, DNA, and spirit. The next day, Creator looked upon all created things and saw it was very good and complete. All was set where it should be. Shalom. The perfect day glimpsed in the garden where Creator and creation were in right relationship. It was holy.*

Let's pause at this moment in the creation story and linger. Humanity's uniqueness over all creation is overshadowed only by the magnitude of the seventh day. The day of rest, or sabbath, is not about taking a day off once a week. Rather, it's a snapshot to a time when all things were *right*. Shalom. When God's hope for humanity and creation were *realized*. It's also foreshadowing. At the very start, before the numerous heroes are introduced, before the call to adventure begins, we are given the picture of the ending. The moment without wrongs, only peace, purpose, relationship, and beauty. That's why it was called "very good." Not because each intrinsic element was itself good, but because the relationship between things was right.[1] What was glimpsed in Eden, God promises to reclaim (in a new way), and we cling for the day this dream returns to completeness. Okay, let's jump back in.

*Every good story has a problem, and this one is no different. The Creator sowed a beautiful garden but curiously placed one peculiar tree in the middle and told Adam and Eve not to eat from it. Not long after, the two convened to discuss. Things started to get weird. The snakes were talking now. The three—Adam, Eve, and serpent—decided it was worth the risk to have a bite of the fruit. After all, it looked delicious with its distinct fuchsia color and Jell-O-like consistency. The first bites set off a cataclysmic bang—or perhaps just a whisper— that upset the balance. In that moment, humanity inherited a curse. From their transgressions every human would now be marked "sinner." Not inclined to beauty, but innately distorted so badly that God wouldn't look upon them.*

Let's pause here. Those last two lines don't sound right.

Some Christian doctrines curiously skip the first two chapters of Genesis and jump straight to the third. Systematic theologies even name the progression: creation, fall, redemption. Omitting the first two chapters from the creation narrative has theological impact. For one, there's a stronger case to build surrounding the total depravity of man (noninclusive language used on purpose). Doctrines like "original sin" are drawn from Genesis 3 and the story of the fall. It produces a fundamental identity and nature called "original sinfulness." But we shouldn't skip to the third chapter; instead we should derive our identity from Genesis 1—humanity is rooted in something else: "original goodness." Marked "very good" at the end of the sixth day of creation, humanity is created in God's very own image. This reality is repeated three times, and then a blessing is received. This formative moment speaks loudest to the human condition.

We receive our dignity and value directly from God. That's different from theological persuasions pitting the human origin story around a horrible failure. You likely know well what kind of Christian traditions require this type of formation in order to make sense of the relationship set by a disappointed and angry God. Some will argue that our image-bearing goodness was simply lost at the fall. I contend it was not. Even early Reformed thinkers like John Calvin and Martin Luther didn't argue that humanity no longer bears the image of God. What seems to be at stake is our root nature. Are we predisposed to evil? Or are we fundamentally good? Have you thought about how our root being influences our perception of self and others? In reality, we have the capacity for both, but I contend that the fullness of our humanity is found when we walk in the light. We may not be inherently good (although I'm okay with that argument), but we are certainly formed under inherent image-bearing goodness. This affects the way we view ourselves and those around us.

It changes how we act, too. We don't set out to not do evil things; rather, we are drawn to actively discover the fullness of our image-bearing beauty! Some traditions would shelve this under the pursuit of "holiness," but those traditions often lie stuck with the penitent individual. Living out the fullness of our humanity is an outward action that mimics not only the work of Jesus but also the great commandment. Christians don't embody the rule of "Don't do unto others as you wouldn't have done to you"; rather, we "love one another as you love yourself." Big difference. Back to our story.

*The first bites set off a cataclysmic bang—or perhaps just a whisper—that upset the balance. Something broke and the consequences were immediate. The people were expelled from the garden, and they lost more than the relationship with the land. They lost their unique relationship with Creator, too. Where did Creator go? In a demonstration of love, Creator left the garden, chasing after the banished and longing for a return to the garden. That dream for a return was unwavering. The hope is to reconcile creation to a place where all things are well and right again.*

*As stories go, problems arose, and in this case it was because people are forgetful. Busy with self-interests. Memories fade and stories change. It didn't take long until most forgot Creator's dream. Like the time a tower was built to reach the sky. It didn't go so well. Things actually got worse— much worse. Humanity was taken through inexplicable loss. The world wiped out in a flood. Was it a rash choice? Yes. Creator spoke, "Let us start things again." A new family, same hope, same call: remember the dream. From Babel to Noah and Lot, the dream nearly disappeared again. What if instead of a family, a chosen people appeared? What if these people were given the task to usher in Creator's dream? So a promise was given to both Abraham and Hagar. Each would have a son, and each would be blessed with a multitude of descendants as numerous as the stars. And to Abraham, an invitation.*

*His blessing—to be counted as part of God's family—would extend to all people too.*

The way we read the Bible matters. How we understand and interact with the overarching narrative is crucial. Which narrative you choose is the question. God's dream to reconcile and redeem all things is the main plotline from Genesis to Revelation. How people, nations, prophets, and kings deal with this dream is the ongoing saga. Our job is to identify the cohesive elements that intricately connect the story. Abraham's blessing, or covenant, is one. The covenant between God and Abraham is held in the collective memory of the Israelites. It's one that Jesus expands when the Holy Spirit becomes the future mark to Abraham's blessing expanding to all people. Not for a multitude of descendants, but the invitation to be part of God's family. That promise extends to us, by faith, in the present (Acts 7; Galatians 3). Back to our story.

*A new tribe emerged yet the rhythm repeated. Hope of justice, beauty, and love waned. The tribe forgot their purpose and did what was right in their own eyes, fell away, and got into trouble. Other nations grew strong, and the people were left by the wayside—in fact, now they were enslaved. You may have heard about these stories. A band of brothers sold their younger sibling to Egypt and returned years later for food, only to discover the brother leading the king's court. Or the one about a young Hebrew boy who grew up in Pharaoh's household as a prince. The boy grew into a young man, and one day tried to enact justice from his own hand. He murdered another and escaped into hiding for his remaining days, or so he thought. His exile spanned days into years, years into decades, when finally, from afar, Creator heard the cries of the enslaved people. Moses was called to share the hope for liberation. Miraculous signs and wonders put the plan in motion.*

*The sky began to fall—the* sky *began to rain fire! The lone voice of Moses said, "Let us escape now." The initial dash was fast and furious, but no sooner were they away than the formerly enslaved complained. "Why did we choose this? We will never cross the vast sea to escape." Some even wanted to go back! How quickly people forget. But Creator delivered. The miraculous, the improbable, a moment in time to memorialize when the seas parted and the nation escaped and won their freedom.*

*This budding nation without land wandered the desert sands. Time passed on, and days turned into years and years into four decades. They wandered aimlessly at times, but through their cries, another promise was born. What is a nation without a growing identity? From the mountaintop a new way outlined in a law. With tablets in hand, and a chosen land found, the nation of Israel got its start to bear Creator's dream. Be the host of ushering in the time and space where all wrongs turn right, where justice, beauty, hope, and love are restored, where the garden is reclaimed and all can be well.*

*But as stories go, problems arose, and the Creator watched as the nation forgot its purpose. People did what was right in their own eyes, fell away, got into trouble, cried out to Creator; Creator relented and delivered them. The same rhythm over and over again. Maybe the answer was to have a king or two? Some did pretty well, some expanded the territory, many did not. But as kings do, they sought to do what was right in their own eyes and not what Creator had hoped. Prophets tried to call the nation back, but they still fell away, lost their land, regained it, only to lose it again one final time, all while God stood aside waiting for someone to remember the story about the garden.*

*Then came a time when it seemed apparent that the nation would never usher in Creator's ultimate hope. The prophets began to speak of a different return. A King again, but not just any king, a faithful King who would upend all kingships. A messiah was foretold, one that would liberate the people, but not in the manner they would expect. A savior would fulfill and inaugurate the Creator's dream for a return to the garden, here on earth, an age when all things would be back to being right.*

*Our story reaches its climax with a whimper. A small babe was born into the chaos of a family gathered for a required census. The child was born in relative mystery. Apart from his mother, few knew about the kind of deliverance he would offer. The first years of life were spent as a refugee escaping tyranny. Although there are scant details about his life until his final years, what we do have draws us into a life that transcends the history of humanity. A life that transcends history? What makes him so special? His character did not match that of a shrewd king, but rather that of a humble servant. What good is a messiah if there is no triumph? What good is the claim for salvation if a king can't liberate his people? Unless this liberation is much wider than one can possibly imagine.*

\*    \*    \*

Humanity is created in the very image of God, but oftentimes it is a struggle to walk into this beauty. Some would call the impediments withholding this reclamation "sin." Sin as both an individual condition and a holistic problem. This means in many ways, liberation is not something we can claim on our own. We need liberation from the systems and powers seeking to make us less whole. That's particularly true for bodies on the margins.

This truth doesn't remove our agency, but it does highlight how some face greater systemic barriers to ultimate freedom. Which means that when it comes to sin, it's not so much about inheriting an underlying condition or breaking moral codes. Rather, sin reflects missing the mark, distorting our image-bearing humanity with cheap substitutes. We are designed for belonging and to flourish in our bodies. Our purpose is to continuously reclaim this image, bearing witness to our new humanity here on earth. It happens when we live out the fullness of our image-bearing humanity. When I speak of liberation, I'm referring to the reclamation of this reality. And here's the connection—Jesus inaugurates this reality. The dream that God has for creation comes alive in Jesus. What the heroes of the faith, and the nation of Israel, could not achieve in announcing the totality of God's reign on earth, Jesus completes.

We pause here to make two important points serving as critical junctions for unpacking faith. First, the *way* of Jesus has profound implications in the present. To discern what this way entails is our work, and many traditions miss the mark. Second, at the cross and subsequent resurrection, *something* happens that alters the course of history. So much can be explored around these two points, so our brief foray will only be a taste.

## FIRST SHALL BE LAST

Jesus is the climactic hero in the biblical narrative. It serves us to take seriously how we may understand the breadth of God's story through him. That means interpreting the Bible "through the eyes and nature of Jesus" and deriving our understandings through the lens of the spirit and ethic of him.[2] It also means the life and teachings of Jesus can define our character and faith today. There are obvious foundations to begin with. It's shared both triumphantly and transparently that the greatest of all the commands from Jesus is love. We have already immersed ourselves into the magnitude of this calling. Love God, our neighbor, one another, and ourselves. Love is not merely an ethic to adhere to, but an embodied choice to pursue.

There's that word again, *embody*. I've used it a lot to refer to our bodies and the way we can understand and interact with ideas across all our senses. We must take on the challenge ourselves to feel in our gut and bones what it means to love and be loved. We make imperfect attempts at love because we have been so graciously given God's outpouring love in creation and on the cross. From this root the Christian life seeks to adopt, or in fact embody both individually and communally, the way of Jesus. We can find the gospel accounts (Matthew, Mark, Luke, and John) full of stories, and the other books in the New Testament as the important additions. Further still, we can single out the obvious and crucial teachings. They are found in the fifth chapter of Matthew's gospel in the Beatitudes, or the Sermon on the Mount. Here we discover what the subversive way of Jesus tangibly looks like.

Blessed[3] are those who recognize their need for God, for the kingdom of heaven is yours.

Blessed are those who grieve all that ain't right in the world, for you will be comforted.

Blessed are people who show graciousness, for you will inherit the earth.

Blessed are those who hunger and thirst for justice, for you will be fed until full.

Blessed are people who show mercy, for you will receive mercy.

Blessed are the peacemakers, for you will be called God's children.

Blessed are those who are hounded for the sake of justice, for theirs is the kingdom of heaven.[4]

What's shocking to me is how these teachings remain antithetical to modern-day social structures two thousand years later. When I read the Beatitudes, I'm always struck with something new. Not only how they convict, but also how those who are hurting find comfort, and those who are on the margins are promised liberation. To be more specific, people on the margins are brought to the center, a consistent and distinct feature in Jesus' ministry. The last shall be first and the first last (Luke 13:30), famous words of Jesus and ones echoed by others throughout history. Theorist Frantz Fanon built his thesis around this teaching in his book *The Wretched of the Earth*, but unlike the philosophy of Fanon, who considered the sword as a means to liberation, the way of Jesus is distinctly nonviolent.

I don't think we're supposed to arrive at a degree of perfection, but these verses outline the activity—the outward pursuit—of our faith. Does your church community, or any community for that matter, reflect these practices? Do you see yourself reflected in any of these verses? This is a useful tool when reading through the gospel accounts. Whom do you identify with in the stories? What speaks directly to you?

I marvel at the ways that Jesus upends patriarchy. Women announce Jesus before he is even born. It is the women at the tomb who are the first evangelists of the resurrection. Women are given prominent voice, name, healing, space, leadership in the inner circle of disciples (and later the church), and even spar with (and best) Jesus on theological teachings (see Mark 7:24–29). All of this in an age where women were considered property. When we read the stories and take seriously the direction Jesus puts in front of us—the way to find fullness of life and liberation—how we picture ourselves in the stories matters.

To be like Jesus is to embody traits that upend cultural systems, particularly when they come from religious institutions. The harshest words of condemnation ever spoken by Jesus are reserved for some choice groups of people. Those who are rich and who exploit others to get rich. And the religious leaders and elite. Religious leaders were chastised for maintaining systems of marginalization that exploited the least. Jesus even upends the temple market in protest. He deplores interpretation of scriptures that retain power structures and vilifies their abuse of power. *Abuse* is the choice word.

When contemporary Christians identify with biblical characters, we tend to associate with Jesus or any hero protagonists. Christians don't read themselves as the potential villains in the stories. We don't consider how the church today mimics the religious elite surrounding Jesus. It's liberating for Christians on the margins—which is the central point—to discover Jesus continuously siding *with* the margins. This posture is prevalent and constant. Jesus to the poor, the spiritually infirmed, the mentally abused, the destitute, the broken, the sick, the women and children. The margins are drawn closest to Jesus. To draw on the preaching of Otis Moss III and the writings of Howard Thurman, Jesus through the lens of the disinherited is a different Jesus.

Jesus changes the course of history by inaugurating God's throne of justice on earth through a fundamental act of nonviolence. It's in Jesus where we see our Messiah—Savior to the world—who was and is and is to come. Who became human, was crucified, suffered and was buried, but triumphed in the end, declaring victory over the power of all that ain't right in the world by rising on the third day. I want more of this Jesus, and I fail at living into my part. But it's not shame driving me forward but rather the ceaseless love and constant invitation to come back again to find liberation and wholeness.

## ATONE

Connecting the pieces to simple yet profound theological questions can help us figure out what to discard and what to keep. One final question may serve us in the process of deconstruction and reclamation: Why did Jesus have to die? Both death on the cross and subsequent resurrection—what does it do? This is a huge question that sits at the very core of the Christian faith. The Sunday school answer is of course quite simple: Jesus died for our sins. We've lingered around a reorientation on what sin is. Not the inherited condition associated with breaking moral codes, but an inherited condition to blunder in our pursuit to live out the fullness of our image-bearing beauty. But what does *death* actually accomplish?

Atonement is how the work of Jesus puts humanity, and beyond, into right relationship with God. Some traditions spend a lot of time on the cross, accentuating blood and gore to match a bloodthirsty and wrathful God. Angry God requires a violent sacrifice for appeasement. Without the right violent sacrifice, God will in turn permit eternal violence and wrath on your body and soul. This perspective is not for me. But it sure works to scare a lot of people into compliance. Fear is a tiresome motivator, and one that ironically does not grant life.

This satisfaction motif falls apart when the aspect of violence becomes divinely inspired. A violent God goes against the character of Jesus in every way and completely undermines the nonviolent resolution of the cross as exemplified through Christ's obedience to a nonviolent way even in death. The substitutionary theory, which is similar to satisfaction theory, only with added legalistic framework to match the times during the Reformation, considers the death of Jesus a legal discharge "of the sinner's legal status before God but says nothing about a transformed life."[5] It also twists the conditions of what godly justice looks like.

There are many theories of atonement, including the following:

- Ransom theory, where the devil is bested to release humanity from the bondage of death (the devil never has such magnitude of power).
- Moral influence theory, where Jesus dies as a symbol of God's profound love, or a belief that the honor of God had to be protected.
- Satisfaction theory, to appease the violent rage of a wrathful God.
- Substitutionary theory, which appeases another angry God looking to punish someone, anyone, for humanity's sin.
- Penal substitutionary theory, which turns Jesus into a coin in a cosmic transaction to fulfill a debt obligation, which is oddly capitalistic.

Now, I'm hardly giving each of these theories of atonement the attention to match the accumulated thought over the course of church history. You can find Bible verses to support a position in each. But at the end of the day, all we have are theories, and we ought to draw near to the ones that grant life and were reflected in the early church.

The early church spent little time arguing over theories, but they did adopt a position that's related to what some call "narrative *Christus Victor*." Within, "the death of the cross is anything but a loving act of God; it is the product of the forces of evil opposing the reign of God. . . . Jesus' death is not a loving act of God, but the ultimate statement that distinguishes the rule of God from the reign of evil."[6] God didn't orchestrate this death, people did. And the death of Jesus is the culmination of all powers both seen and unseen who reject God's dream and oppose God's rule. The early church had a visceral connection to this reality. When the temple veil tore in two, something shifted within the actual world of space, time, and matter. They, like us, were the recipients of a new gift of forgiveness. Let's read a summation by N. T. Wright:

> The "forgiveness of sins" was neither simply a personal experience nor a moral command. . . . It was the name for a new state of being, a new world, the world of resurrection . . . the moment the prison door is flung open. . . . A fact rooted in the one-off accomplishment of Jesus's death, then revealed in his resurrection, and then put to work through the Spirit in the transformed lives of his followers. . . . It would come to mean "new covenant" and "new creation." The gospel was the announcement of this new reality.[7]

Resurrection must go together with crucifixion. There is no beauty, no solution, no salvation, without triumph and victory over all that ain't right in the world. If the greatest disconnection to our existence—that is, death and all it represents—cannot be overcome, then there is no liberation. Jesus defeats all the powers seeking to make us, and creation, less whole by "dealing with the sins, the human idolatries and injustices, that handed to the 'powers' the authority and responsibility given to humans in the first place."[8] Our calling is to carry on this vocation and preview the unfolding kingdom hope in the here and now. Resurrection is the reason and proof for new creation and the possibilities to fully pursue the fullness of our humanity under the new power and reign of God.[9] The example is he who laid his life down for his friends (John 15:13). The atoning act, with subsequent resurrection, not only inaugurated this reign but restored humanity into God's creative purpose to put all things into right relationship, just as in the garden, only this time it will be in the new garden found in the new city (Revelation 21–22). We can make this rule visible in the here and now. When we take seriously the Lord's Prayer, we pray for "thy kingdom come, on earth as it is in heaven." The inbreaking kingdom in its fullness now, made visible through the confrontation to all that ain't right in the world, like the powers and forces seeking to make those on the margins less whole.

To end this chapter, we turn to the conclusion of our story.

*     *     *

*For three days it was done. For three days we lost.*

*Darkness again.*

*Then the miraculous, the improbable, a triumph over all things that ain't right. On the third day light pierced through the dark. The beginning story of the first seven days replayed in a shorter three.*

*On the third day a group of women went down to the tomb so they could anoint his body with spices. The tomb was at the back of a garden, and as they turned the final bend they stopped in bewilderment. The tomb was open and the guards nowhere to be seen. One lonely soul in the garden wept. She barely noticed another figure from the corner of her eye.*

*He approached and asked, "Why are you crying?"*

*Thinking he was the gardener she replied, "They took him . . ."*

*Jesus looked and called her by name, "Mary."*
*She turned toward him and cried out.*

The story of the women finding the resurrected Jesus is stunning. Mary thought the risen Lord was the gardener! How fitting that our story began in the garden and ends in the same place. Jesus is a gardener who cultivates life in all who come to him. Gardeners dig into the earth, they transform decay into new life, they tend, and tend, and tend to the soil until it bears fruit. Gardeners spend their lives in seasonal rhythm laying down roots, planting, pulling up weeds, pruning. They can see the possibilities in the seeds before they bloom. They know all the patience and turmoil will one day produce breathtaking beauty. That's what we need in pursuit of our liberation—more beauty.

# 8

# The Yawning Awning

**IN THE BOOK OF ACTS,** chapter 10, there's a story that begins along the Mediterranean. A row of beach houses, each boasting different color awnings along their rooftop terraces, line the shore. It's around lunchtime, and the smells from the day's catch fill the air. Before the meal is served Peter escapes to the terrace for a quick rest. He positions a cushion to face the midday seas and settles in. His eyes draw heavy as his head begins to tip. The sound of the gentle waves begins to pull him to the place just between waking and sleeping. He can hear the flapping awning, but now he can see one too. It's coming toward him, and the awning turns into a large linen sheet being lowered by its four corners. Inside the sheet are all kinds of four-legged animals, reptiles, and wild birds.

A voice in the distance fills the air. "Get up, Peter! Eat!"

Peter responds, "Absolutely not, Lord! I have never eaten anything impure or unclean."

The voice responds, "Never consider unclean what God has made pure."

This happens three more times before Peter is pulled from his dreamlike trance as the rolling sea waves come back into focus.

The peculiar vision likely struck Peter in more ways than one. No doubt he was thinking about the shame of betraying the Lord three times on the morning of the crucifixion. He couldn't forget the three times Jesus graciously welcomed him back by asking him three times, "Do you love me?" Now, as he lies on the terrace in Joppa, the voice of the Lord speaks to him again, three times. Peter is a thinker and will need to process his thoughts. But before he can retire to lunch, he hears a voice again. The Spirit alerts him, "Three people are looking for you, go with them." And so begin the adventures of Peter to the Gentiles.

## FORMATION FROM WITHIN

We start this chapter with formative stories, paying specific attention to the radical inclusivity marking the early church. Once we find our language and bearings, we will end with ways to develop and reclaim formation with influences outside of Christianity too.

Our journey to reclaim pieces of the Christian faith begins by establishing Jesus as the center of God's unfolding story to rescue and redeem all of creation. It's in Jesus, who takes on the embodiment of the new Israel seeking its rebirth, where God's original purpose from the garden is fulfilled. To the average Jewish person, the talk of liberation would include deliverance from Rome. That would be the ultimate success for Israel's new beginning. But that's not what happened. Instead, although the formation of the church at Pentecost was shaped around Jewish believers (Israel), the picture is immediately one of decentering. In Acts 2 everyone hears the good news in their own language. God's intended plan for Israel, fulfilled in Jesus, was set to stretch much wider than Israel. From this shift we can reclaim aspects of Christian formation.

The story of Peter's vision in Joppa happens immediately after an angel gives Cornelius, a Roman centurion, a message to locate Peter. The climax of the chapter happens in Acts 10:34 when Peter is compelled to say, "I'm learning here, learning about the magnitude of our God, who doesn't show partiality to one group of people over another." The significance of his statement, and then what happens in verse 44—the Holy Spirit descends on everyone—is monumental.

In this moment the new reign was confirmed to move beyond the elect people (Israel), expanding to all people. Willie Jennings writes, "The election of Jesus turns Israel's election outwards. . . . [It] does a stunning work by opening the possibilities of boundary-shattering love between strangers and enemies."[1] Initially, the emerging, still Jewish church had trouble with this radical inclusion. They thought if you were a part of this emerging movement you had to be Jewish. The primary issues for belonging were religious. You can read how Peter (through his vision and experience with Cornelius), and later the apostle Paul (who argues with church leaders in Galatians 2:11–21), pull the early Jewish church leaders out of religious exclusivity.

The primary issues were twofold: circumcision and food restrictions. Both (especially the former) were critical identifying features in Judaism. They, however, were *not* going to be critical attributes in early Christianity. Imagine the profound risk for males. To be fully included in the church, you had to—as an adult, using technology from two thousand years ago—get circumcised. Not only were members of the early church facing life-and-death consequences because they were fundamentally opposing the empire (which, by the way, makes the story of Cornelius even more compelling—he's the enemy in the flesh), but they might also die from getting circumcised, which was done just to appease religious ideology.

The way the early church struggled through these early identifying pieces as they learned what to keep and what to discard not only is an exercise in deconstruction, but also gives our church traditions the permission required to reimagine the ways we can be radically inclusive by emulating Jesus.

Theological problems in contemporary Christianity are starkly similar to those in the Acts church. Today two predominant divisions are racial segregation and same-gender marriage. I have already pointed out how commonplace racial segregation remains for most churches. Although there are exceptions to the rule, segregation remains embedded, and few churches have the willingness or the skills to change. For diversity to happen it usually needs be a starting value in a new church because dismantling segregation requires a complete divestment from white hegemony, ranging from individual formation to systemic structures. This change may be too big.

Unlike segregation, the second divisive issue is gaining more traction, particularly in younger generations that view queerness as normative. Progressive churches have led in including the LGBTQIA community and in performing same-gender marriages.[2] Conversely, non-affirming traditions consider the issue to be a matter of fundamental theology and organizational integrity. As we read in chapter 6, the religious right built itself up by stoking fear and naming pariahs. After the failure to stop desegregation, segregation was swapped, under the guise of protecting "family values," for vilification of the emerging gay and lesbian community. Contrast this posture to the way Jesus defines character. Be known by your love for one another and the other. Sounds pretty simple. So how can there be such a wide divergence in theological opinion and praxis? It all comes down to power and how you read the Bible.

For some, affirming queerness and same-gender marriage disobeys their biblical truths. But remember the question we always ask—Whose truths? At these junctures we must dig deep into reclamation by appealing to the early church. Peter and Paul, along with the Jerusalem church, engaged in a deliberative process to determine whether the scriptures were being misused in their contextual situations. Their deliberation reflects a level of community discernment that we can follow. It is one that Jesus champions as well.[3] The old law was processed through how the community related to it, which in turn determined its validity.

In the case of Peter and Paul, the council determined that the commands and work of Jesus—who ultimately came to fulfill the law—overruled religious orders. Circumcision and food purity laws were dropped as requirements to belonging for Gentile believers. How they came to this conclusion speaks to the way Jesus became the operative "lens" through which they understood God's unfolding work in their present. Interpreting scripture must always fit God's culminating hope to restore all things into right relationship. It's here where contemporary issues of theology run into problems. What's to stop denominations or churches from going through a process of discernment and enhancing stringent theological barriers? That's what happened to me. When I gave up my pastoral credentials, a small minority of members stood in vocal opposition, yet the established majority had already made up their mind. In this instance, as with many others, the power holders opted to preserve theological convictions that barred LGBTQIA folks from living out their whole selves. They opted for the old law, slamming shut the door to God's expansive inclusivity and ministry of reconciliation.

In the case of same-gender marriage and affirming LGBTQIA or Two-Spirit folks, there is a pathway outside the traditionalist versus affirming divide. One that celebrates human flourishing over religious orthodoxy. The story starts in Genesis 1. All are created beautiful, profound image bearers of God, and God never makes mistakes. Ever. No amount of causal theological assumptions can circumvent this original truth. What God has affirmed in every LGBTQIA person, in sexuality and gender, is called very good.

What does very good look like? When someone is living into their whole identity and that in turn cultivates whole *health* of mind, body, and spirit. So we don't need to unpack individual scriptures to affirm or deny a theological position here. (If you want to read those books they're out there.) We already know that Jesus inaugurates the new reign of God, paving the way for us to venture toward the fullness of life. We know that the examples of relationship and marriage in scripture emphasize fidelity over the cultural norms that accepted exploitation. Finally, we know that how we understand the stories in the Bible today needs to be discerned in the present. Everyone has to do this contextual work. Therefore, the conclusions we make are determined by who is allowed at the decision-making table, and who stands to lose power. With the margins at the table, a new outlook on goodness can emerge.

## BEDROCK

Does the discernment of scripture by a community mean that any theological position is up for grabs? The multitude of denominations in existence answers this question. The short of it is, yes. Does this mean every doctrinal belief is subjective and every theological insight opinion? Again, yes! That doesn't necessarily mean they all must be discarded, but they certainly are productions of man (usually men), and should always be scrutinized.

Community discernment can lead to malformed theologies and actions. I've already shared my experience in the Vineyard, but look at the history of whiteness and white supremacy too. Look at the individual churches today with an ardent anti-vax stance, bringing harm into the church and into the neighborhood. Count the voices of those who adopt white supremacist activities (the softer version is called white nationalism) and build dividing walls to ensure marginalized bodies are excluded. There's an alarming ease of turning Jesus into our own image rather than the other way around. We know the difference because the former produces bad fruit.

If any opinion counts, that leaves us with another question. Is there any "nonnegotiable truth" in the Christian faith? As in, if denominations had to make a list of "must-haves," what would be on it? Is it the doctrinal statement? A laundry list of theological positions? Most of us would have to search for a particular statement of beliefs to know what's on it, although we're probably familiar with key pieces. The trinity of God the Father, Son, and Holy Spirit. Something about the Bible (more on this later). Some will even include positions on end times, marriage, spiritual gifts, and so forth. Oftentimes the list implicitly reveals what a tradition is *against*. Which is kind of sad when you think of it. Christians are often understood by what they oppose rather than by how they give life.[4] The list of these "truths" can be lengthy.

So are there nonnegotiables? In societies rooted in rugged individualism, and therefore truth as defined by the individual, the notion of universal truths is scoffed at. Individuals can have a set of fundamental beliefs; just don't push them on other people. It's a kind of "don't ask, don't tell" policy of religion. So is that it? Is truth subjective? And if we can discern truth through community, as evidenced in the New Testament when interacting with Old Testament laws, is everything up for grabs? These are important questions of deconstruction because where you land dictates what you reclaim.

As we've discussed, walking away from it all, including any claims to objective truth, is another pathway. This alternative, however, eventually leaves one staring into an abyss. Which is to say, we should aspire to fill our human longings with *something*. I haven't found an alternative to Jesus, but some do try. As a proponent of reclamation, I believe there are fundamentals in the Christian faith worth hanging on to. How they are interpreted and understood, however, is unique to context. That reality is a beautiful result of the first—and perhaps only—truth to keep: incarnation.

The incarnation, Jesus as fully God, fully human, along with his ministry and teachings, his sacrifice to take the sins of the world unto death on the cross, and his subsequent defeat of those powers in resurrection, is the one nonnegotiable. When deconstruction eventually hits bedrock, that base layer of truth is the incarnate Christ. It's the truth we need—to know God is with us. Incarnation is God contextualizing into the history of humanity in order to be known. This act means Jesus can be contextualized (understood) within any cultural and temporal context. God is knowable because we can look at Jesus to know what God looks like. Jesus is worth reclaiming because in him we discern and form our character and build our community.

Pragmatically, what does this look like? The must-haves in action are what Jesus values. Love, justice, beauty, and hope. The radical inclusivity that Jesus practiced, by bringing the marginalized to the center, is our marker. A distinctly triune demonstration of unity in diversity in action through practices of inclusivity and hospitality. In the search for full belonging, we must learn to embody these things in the context of healthy community. We can discern the details through the teachings of Jesus (like the Sermon on the Mount) and watch for the virtues of the Spirit (Galatians 5:22–23; Ephesians 4:2; Colossians 3:12–15) and ask, "Do I (or we) look like these things?" As we discern what to keep and what to discard, reclamation begins on this foundation of incarnation. Everything after is subject to debate.

## FOR (THAT GUY'S) BIBLE TELLS ME SO

There is one more paradox to engage before we move forward. Our picture of Jesus and the early church primarily comes from the Bible. Nearly every Christian tradition claims to take the Bible seriously. Each will produce a picture of who they think Jesus is. Trouble emerges when contextualization occurs within social orders rooted in power. White Jesus emulates the construction of whiteness and the powers and privileges associated with it. On the other hand, the very nature of incarnation means that God is knowable—translatable to place and time. So how do we determine what "the right reading of the Bible" is? It all comes down to our approach to interpretation.

I actually have an allergy to the phrases "because the Bible says so" and "the biblical position is. . . ." What that really means is "*My interpretation* of the Bible says. . . ." When your interpretation is *the* interpretation or the *only* interpretation, we have a problem. Interpretation must be approached with humility. This is why, for me at least, the way we understand preaching, popularized during the Reformation and passed down ever since, falls flat. We don't need a sermon fifty-two weeks of the year to tell us what to think or believe. Rather, we need a shared approach to discern the Scriptures in the here and now. How we can discover what a deeper, more full life in Christ might look like. How the Bible calls us to spot, celebrate, and participate in God's unfolding rescue plan for all of creation. How the community can join together and live out what radical inclusivity looks like in our age.

I find biblical interpretation both infuriating and fascinating. Infuriating because only certain voices are regarded as qualified enough to interpret and guide Christians forward. Fascinating because it's clear, to me at least, the Bible is written by and for people on the margins. It's therefore a story where the primary subjects in God's view to rescue and redeem start with people on the margins to reclaim first. So let's do it—let's reclaim the stories in the Bible.

But first a pragmatic question: *Whose* Bible should we reclaim? I mean literally which translations. If you have a small group of people who each read a different translation, you will always have variation. Does this bother you? It should for the inerrancy proponents. Biblical inerrancy is a modern construction built alongside the rise of modernism, although it was not fully taken on by fundamentalists until it became a tool for patriarchy. Underneath the adoption of inerrancy was a "proxy fight over gender" that upheld the unfolding "politicized commitment to female submission."[5] Inerrancy takes the Bible into a space it wasn't intended to go. It's true, God is without error. But the Bible? It certainly is inspired revelation pointing to Jesus. But is it on par with God? (In this way, sayings like "the *Word* of God," in reference to the Bible, miss a critical nuance.)

Although revelation can be sacred and can include scripture, the terminology has been carelessly employed. The Word (especially in John 1) is Jesus. Full stop. I'm okay with saying the Bible is completely infallible—which means trustworthy—but inerrant? It's not required. Any understanding or training in textual criticism or original languages can attest. Or just pull out those translations and read the differences yourself. The inerrancy crowd will try to get out of this conundrum by saying the "original autographs" were the ones without error. But again, this is a product of doctrine—an opinion—and not one taken on by scripture or the early church.[6] So back to the question, Whose Bible translation can we trust?

I've already lamented the roots of white hegemony in Western Christianity. White men have produced the framework for how we think and believe. The problem? The vast majority of English translations, up until recently, were translated by white men. When we consider that every translating team and every publisher has its own motives for translating the Scriptures, the implications alter meaning. Bias is inevitable given the nature of textual criticism, understanding cross-cultural references, making sense of nuance, and contextualizing interpretation over two thousand years.

Have you ever thought about how interpreter and publisher motivations influence translations? Some translations take the posture of "We want to translate every word as accurately to the original text as possible," and you get a clunky translation like the New American Standard Bible. Others are the exact opposite, trying to put entire thoughts into contemporary English, like the New Living Translation. Some are more devoted to scholars and pastors, like the New Revised Standard Version. Some translators set out to reflect theological positions (conservative or fundamentalist, for example). The English Standard Version is a prime example, and we can include the King James Version as well. Others want to uphold worldview and to license name recognition for profit. MacArthur, Ryrie, and any Bible with a celebrity recommendation are entrenched in this category. Sometimes you get an attempt to translate the Bible into modern vernacular (*The Message*), and other times you get attempts to update relatively good translations but are driven back because conservatives would stop buying your products (Zondervan and the fiasco with the Today's New International Version ). Where does that leave us?

I like N. T. Wright's suggestion (and his New Testament translation) that every generation should retranslate the Scriptures into their vernacular. Ultimately, no single translation is perfect—none can be, as to reflect every nuance to a specific community is impossible. This is why the importance of community discernment can't be understated. Community combined with some skills and tools in translation will go a long way to venture through the Bible well. That combination is my approach. I have enough original language training to read my way through Greek and Hebrew (more so the former). I make my own translations in conjunction with popular translations, including the NIV, NLT, and CEB. The Common English Bible, notably, is part of a growing minority of Bibles that include diverse translator teams. I have also grown fond of Sarah Ruden's *The Gospels: A New Translation*.

What are the implications between translations? This may not be readily acknowledged by traditions with a high view of Scripture, but the Bible takes on different meaning depending on who is interpreting it.

- For centuries, the apostle Junia (Romans 16:7), a woman, was intentionally mistranslated as the masculine Junias to affirm Christian patriarchy.

- *Marriage* and *wife* are inserted into the Hebrew text for words that mean something else.[7]
- How convenient it was for King James to ensure that Matthew 5:39 stated, "Do not resist evil," when the text clearly says, "Do not use violence to resist." He didn't want those peasants to get any ideas.
- Song of Solomon 1:5 wouldn't dissociate being black or dark skinned with beauty (KJV and ESV). "I am black, but comely," versus, "Dark am I, and lovely".
- From the Sermon on the Mount, and throughout the Gospels, we use *righteousness* more often than *justice*. They are the same word in Greek, but most translations use the former, which presents a more individualistic understanding of salvation over a collective activity towards liberation.

I've mentioned only five instances where translations vary widely and shift our picture of God and even ourselves all according to who's doing the interpreting. How many more are there? And more importantly, does this imply we can't trust anything we read? I don't think so. Rather, in the words of Esau McCauley, "I propose . . . we adopt a posture of Jacob and refuse to let go of the text until it blesses us. Stated differently, we adopt a hermeneutic of trust in which we are patient with the text in the belief when interpreted properly it will bring blessing and not a curse."[8]

Even the most committed translators and scholars can't make themselves devoid of influence and formation. Racism, imperialism, and white supremacy are reflected in formative theologies, doctrines, and in Bible translations too. This doesn't mean we can't reclaim the Bible, but it does suggest that the pathway of reclamation means escaping institutional whiteness and patriarchy.

## DECOLONIZING CHRISTIANITY

Deconstructing and dismantling institutional power structures that marginalize has been the bulk of my ministry work for nearly twenty years. Initially it started as a foray into mission, but my focus eventually swayed to belonging and dismantling old church formation. This evolution required new supporting framework for faith, theology, and worldview. In my search I started investing time into decolonizing Christianity. Like other terms emanating from marginalized people groups (like *wokeness*), I had enough awareness to do some due diligence and not, ironically, colonize decolonization. I opted to search out some source material to learn.

Decolonization fundamentally must appeal to teachings of Indigenous People and ways of being that are specific to the land you're situated on. *Land* and *People* are the two operative words. Indigenous teachings and spiritual practices are unique to the stories rooted in specific places and tribes. There is no monolith. That said, there are some commonalities. To think of decolonization is to consider what life was like before colonization. How societies were formed, shaped, and led. How economies and perceptions of ownership and land were viewed. In what manner relationships, to one another and to the land once again, worked intrinsically together rather than as fragmented parts. The Indigenous way of life and how to understand life offers a working alternative to the Western ideas of capitalism, free-market enterprise, private ownership, white supremacy, anti-immigration, nationalism, and rugged individualism, to name a few. What I couldn't see from the onset of my journey was how much of my thinking was rooted in forms of Western imperialism.

In typical Western fashion, I wanted to find answers. The right answers rooted in the right places, but answers nonetheless. I was looking for a booklist. Don't get me wrong, booklists are a great place to start, but they don't have the answers. We need to go deeper. (If only we could achieve reconciliation through booklists!)

As I became more intentional with decolonizing Christianity, I asked Indigenous teachers I knew for direction. One of my old seminary professors, Ray Aldred, was in town speaking at a Rights Relations event. I thought this would be a good chance to reconnect and get some direction for my search. I was seeking a pathway not only to decenter theological whiteness, but where BIPOC Christians could ground liberation as well. I asked Ray, "Can you point me to some key resources on decolonizing Christianity?" He half listened to my inquiry but didn't seem in much of a hurry to give me an answer. I think he asked me a completely unrelated question—probably something about the weather. I was surprised. These weren't the answers I was looking for. Thankfully, Ray didn't leave me hanging. In a kind of nonchalant "you should pay close attention to know how profound this is going to be" way, he offered a suggestion: "You should talk to Tony." That was it.

I vaguely knew about Tony Snow. He still runs different Indigenous ministries at a couple of United Church of Canada churches in my city. Tony is from Morley, just outside of Banff. He is part of the Stoney Nakoda Nation and comes from the line of chiefs. I visited Tony, and after exchanging some stories, I said, "Hey, I'm digging into decolonization, I want to do this right, can you point me to the voices, books, thinkers, leaders on this topic?" But Tony didn't answer me either! Thankfully, he didn't leave me hanging. "You should come to this service I do," he said. "It's part of the Urban Indigenous Church I started. We're reclaiming Indigenous spirituality for Indigenous people." Sure, I thought. Whatever I need to do. Plus, I'm a sucker for visiting unique church plants.

My own church plant is different from the typical run-of-the-mill plant most would be familiar with. We don't meet every week. I'll share more later, but our rhythm before COVID-19 was a larger gathering once a month. Tony's church met once a month too. My partner (Alyssa) and I started to visit Tony's church. They met midafternoon on a Sunday, tucked behind the main sanctuary of an inner-city church. We were welcomed into this tiny community, mostly people from the Stoney Nation, to not merely observe, but participate too. What we encountered and absorbed . . . it's hard to put into words. Services were held in English and in the Stoney language. Prayers were in Stoney. Traditional ways and spiritual exercises were celebrated, tied to either the church calendar or the four seasons.

We watched as elders reclaimed their old practices, outlawed by the government and vilified by the church for over a century. We had no expectations coming in, but we nonetheless received a profound gift. I remember one Sunday in particular. The group ended the service with a traditional hymn sung in their own language. As they raised their voices, time drew still. We sensed something beyond ourselves happening in our midst. As the hymn drew to a close the lingering pause was met with a sense that the room was filled with the presence of more people. I'll never forget the truth-telling that happened next. Philomene sobbed through words tying both lament and liberation together, "I see them! I see them around us!" She explained, "We were never allowed to sing our traditional hymns, but as we sung, I saw the ancestors singing along with us." Philomene wasn't being metaphorical. She saw her ancestors. It gave life to what I could not see, but definitely *felt* in that moment.

It was through the shared wisdom in the Urban Indigenous Church where the profound story of reconciliation was embodied.[9] Reconciliation is not a process of right *thinking*. It's more than putting up an orange or black square on social media. That's performance. Reconciliation requires presence to engage in the repair of broken relationships. My search for answers was found through an invitation to participate in the possibilities discovered through relationship. We received far more than we expected, from a community that should be the last to freely give more. And I remember . . . the last shall be first.

\* \* \*

In our search for true belonging, we must locate suitable alternatives to divest from white supremacy and Christian supremacy. In my own search, three sources have stood out. I have shared about the first in my encounter with the vibrant Ethiopian Orthodox church. This experience catalyzed my deconstruction and subsequent journey to reclaim Christianity. We can learn from Christian traditions older than the Roman Catholic Church. The wisdom in their teachings contained within their histories provides insight displaying a different way of being and believing.

The second appeals to Indigenous spirituality and land-based teaching. Land-based learning includes cultural and spiritual practices of the First Peoples in your region, providing a way of being and understanding before colonization. When we speak to decolonization, of a way before colonization, the answers are discovered here.

Lastly, there is authority emanating from church traditions that have embodied *resistance* to white hegemony in their foundation. African American churches are the primary example in North America, a church that developed outside of white institutional power by necessity. When we seek voices that can draw us to unique perspectives about the marginalized Jesus, this perspective is encapsulated in the African American church tradition. Deep care and attention is spent to unravel God's biblical revelation that centers around holistic liberation. By holistic I mean a liberation that's not contained within the typical Western Christian lens of rugged individualism of individual souls to spend eternity in the clouds. Rather, it is a liberation of mind, body, and spirit, in *this* age and in the age to come. A liberation that can be touched, felt, heard, seen, in the here and now, and one for which we await final deliverance in the future.

I was fortunate enough to have the privilege to fly to Ethiopia and absorb the traditions. That's not available to all. In Canada, there are few churches birthed out of the African diaspora that resemble Black church traditions seen in America. We also share a border with the United States, not Mexico, and therefore South American immigration is far less, and the influence of the "Brown Church"[10] less as well. In my place on the land, I have fewer opportunities to find influence from African American church traditions, liberation or abuelita theology, or womanist theology. In their place, I pay closer attention to the Indigenous voices on Treaty 7 (and beyond).

## DECOLONIZE, DIVEST, DISMANTLE, RECLAIM

Actively decolonizing, divesting, and dismantling the cultural power of whiteness creates the space needed to accommodate new imagination on faith and belonging. How this looks in practice depends on your orientation to the land. Are you a white settler? Then you need to dismantle and divest from white supremacy. Are you a Black, Asian, Latino/a, or other person of color? You need to decolonize. Are you Indigenous? You need to reclaim your ways.

You probably noticed my omission. White folks can't decolonize. You can't decolonize from something you inherit. Of course, if you are white, nobody is calling you a coloni*zer*; instead, it's just to say that you are a prime benefactor of colonization. When we speak to social structures including whiteness, we understand that the privileges are *bestowed*. They can't be denied. You may not, as a white person, dissent from receiving a wrongful inheritance. You can, however, actively *divest* from what is automatically given. You can choose, when you see it, to reject and rebel against the power system that simultaneously benefits you.

Because white folks are benefactors of systemic power, another primary activity you can lead is *dismantling* the systems. Dismantling white supremacy, Western imperialism, and all things associated must be led by those with cultural and institutional power. For white folks, your prime responsibility should be to dismantle the power systems you inherit. (That's not to say white people have all the power, but when it comes to institutional and systemic power, they hold most of it.) This is not to say any one of us can undo the systemic problems associated with the legacy of colonization. But as Christians, we are called to the ministry of reconciliation (2 Corinthians 5:11–21). It is work toward justice and the overturning of systems of sin undermining all from living out their whole selves. Which is a fitting way for us to end this chapter. A reminder of who God is and what God values.

God is a God of justice (Isaiah 30:18) who loves justice (Isaiah 61:8) and whose foundation is justice (Psalms 11:7; 97:2), which means God reviles any injustice (Isaiah 58). It is the work of Jesus to bring justice to the nations (Isaiah 42:1), a reflection of the very identity of God (Jeremiah 9:24). Our commandment is to establish justice (Ezekiel 45:9), let justice roll down like waters of an ever-flowing stream (Amos 5:24), do justice as we embrace faithful love, and walk humbly (Micah 6:8). Jesus exhorts us to hunger and thirst for justice, calling any—especially religious people who should know better—terrible if justice and love are neglected. If love is the great commandment, justice is what this love looks like in public (to use the words of Cornel West). Justice is to bring broken things into right relationship. This takes place after the repair of all that has been broken. It's not reserved solely for work between people but is a foundation to the Christian faith to bring about the liberation of entire oppressive systems too.

As we reclaim new ways of being and understanding faith, there are plain foundations we can grasp in a reclaimed biblical text—ironically, a plain reading of what God values. To dismantle, divest, decolonize, and reclaim the kingdom *now* in our midst is to participate in the unfolding hope and dream to put the world to rights. May it be so—imperfectly—for you and your crew.

# 9

# Know Thyself

**BEFORE THE ADVENT** of online streaming I went through a big Jackie Chan phase. Most of his movies were filmed in China, and dubbed versions were available only on VHS tape. Blockbuster rarely carried foreign films from China, so when I stumbled across countless tapes of old Jackie Chan movies, I was in heaven. Jackie jumped through buildings, windows, pinball machines, bamboo scaffolding, anything really. I remember one film in particular called *Who Am I?* (我是誰). After suffering from a bout of temporary amnesia Jackie stands at the top of a building overlooking the city and screams into the void, "Who am I?! Who am I?!" I've thought about his words at times, probably more deeply than they were intended. Do I even know who I am?

In his memoir, *Born a Crime*, comedian Trevor Noah deftly describes the absurdity of race categories. He is biracial, with a white dad and a Black mom, a union once deemed illegal in his native land of South Africa. During apartheid, individuals were assigned a status that was also printed on an ID card. There were different race categories: black, colored, and white. (Additional categories were added later.) Black was considered the lowest on the unwritten scale and white the best.

Noah and I are about the same age, so I pictured myself growing up in South Africa and noticed another level of absurdity. As Noah described the system he noted that if you did not fall within one of the categories, you weren't automatically dumped into the catchall "colored." Rather, determination was arbitrary. For instance, Japanese people were considered white because there were economic advantages for the South African government to gain favor with Japan. Chinese people, on the other hand, are not Japanese, so they were initially classified as colored.

So in this world dominated by white supremacy, I would, in all my multiethnic glory, fit into all three. I assume white must be some overarching category—like multiplying anything by zero, multiplying by white results in white. In old apartheid South Africa I guess I'd be white? Obviously, the absurdity of race wouldn't play out that way—I'd likely fall into whichever *non*-white category I looked most like, which in the South African sun would be dark brown. The absurdity of race constructs obviously has more nefarious outcomes. One of the sad realities is how some people accept race definitions to describe their personhood at the expense of losing memories of their own people.

If you've ever been to a run-of-the-mill church conference that's not specifically ethnic (e.g., the Chinese Winter Conference), then you know these spaces are overwhelmingly white. They are exhausting spaces to navigate for people who don't match the white heteronormative able body. The last one I attended was a small one-day gathering in my city. The theme was new church expressions to match shifting city demographics. In attendance were three people including myself that made up the entire BIPOC contingent. Naturally, we combined during breakouts. I remember one session in particular where the three of us were seated with three others who were white. As we introduced ourselves it happened again. Someone asked me, "What are you?" Great, not this again.

In her book *Mixed Blessing*, Chandra Crane writes about embracing the fullness of multiethnic identity. One way to do so is to resist using the metrics of white supremacy. One such metric is fractional identity. Blood quantum laws employ formulas of certain percentages to dictate race or status. Sometimes fractions are replaced with a "one-drop rule," used to delineate white and Black, where Black is determined by the presence of any Black ancestor in the bloodline.

I've employed an iteration of blood quantum to explain myself. In fact, sometimes I don't even recognize I'm doing it, that's how ingrained this method of explaining identity is. When people ask "What are you?," my reply has often been, "I'm one-half West Indian, one-quarter Japanese, and one-quarter Chinese. These three together ($\frac{1}{2} + \frac{1}{4} + \frac{1}{4} = 1$) make me whole." But I have it all wrong. What part of me is the Chinese part? And which the Japanese? And is it my bottom half that's Trinidadian? In *Mixed Blessing*, Crane liberates multiethnic people from fractional identity by reminding us we are *all* our ethnicities. I am wholly Chinese, as I am Japanese, as I am West Indian. It's $1 + 1 + 1 = 1$. Or if I was cheeky, $1 + 1 + 1 = 3$. How can one person be three? It's an attribute only multiethnic people have, our "superpower," as Crane calls it. We are not mere reflections of; rather, we embody in whole each of our ethnicities. Fractioning identity in a bid to explain how we may belong is an exercise for a white supremacist world. It's not necessary and it's not right.

Although my multiethnic identity is unique, everyone should appeal to ethnicity in the search for belonging. In fact, it's a critical piece in self-discovery because it deepens our understanding of our people while simultaneously subverting the social constructs of race that seek to have us give up our family story in favor of whitewashed and empty versions of self.

When the question "What are you?" rolled around at that church conference, this time my friend cut in—who happened to be Tony from our story earlier. He turned the tables by saying, "That's always a question white people ask. Why don't you tell us where you're from? What are you?!" It doesn't take much cultural awareness to see the bind white people are caught in when an Indigenous person asks them, "Where are you from?" The answer is not "I'm from here," referring to the land. You may have been born here, but how did you and your people arrive? With the tables turned, the older white man stumbled through a surprising response. Usually, people with European ancestry have some idea about their people. Maybe they don't have a full sense of lineage, but they can generally name a country, like "My grandmother is from England and my grandfather is German." But this gentleman sat in stunned silence. "I've never thought about that. I mean, I'm white . . ." It took him a few more moments before he added, "I guess my grandparents have some Scandinavian heritage, but that's all I really know." This man had lived most of his life without anybody asking him where he was from, a phenomenon only a white person in North America could achieve. But more importantly, he started to realize how disconnected he was from his people and his traditions. In that moment, I felt sorry for him. He took on the outside affirmations associated with cultural whiteness that erased his ethnic identity.

To embrace racialization as core identity is to embrace a counterfeit identity. The allure makes sense for whiteness given the privileges it bestows. Yet it remains a fabrication built on a system to hoard power rather than an expression of a particular people connected to a particular land. The categories of race were largely developed in the fifteenth century and the concept has since proliferated across the globe. Given its relatively later construction, we must also note that there are no connections between race as we understand it today and the stories in the Bible. Although God sees the categories from the children's song, red, brown, yellow, black, and white, because we have created them, God does not affirm them. God won't redeem race. God does, however, see and affirm our *ethnicity*. In Revelation 7:9, most translations say that every nation, tribe, people, and language are together standing before the throne. The word *nation* is ēthnos in Greek, from which we derive the English word *ethnicity*. Just as the incarnation makes God knowable within cultural context, so God also affirms and redeems cultures that shape and form us. Which is to say, our ethnicity counts. As race aims to differentiate on the basis of skin tone and proximity to whiteness, ethnicity affirms our whole being as it is attached to our culture, land, and people. As an aside, skin color is never erased. It's part of identity. God sees color. Unless you're blind, affirming someone's skin tone is part of seeing that person. Isn't it incredible that there are so many shades of skin color in the world and that each and every one of them reflects the Creator? This is a mystery, and it's a mystery of beauty.

## LOVE THYSELF

How do we build into our God-given identity? For starters, we need to learn to love thyself, and we can't love thyself in full without first knowing (and accepting) thyself. This constitutes an embodied knowledge that characterizes your entire personhood (or self). Embodiment in this case means a self known through the whole of body, soul, and spirit—pieces that can never be separated.[1] We often don't think of the self as a body; rather, we think of the self as a mind operating that body. It's a level of dualism that fractions off pieces of our personhood. That may seem routine within our Western understanding of self, but it's woefully incomplete. We must, ironically, dissociate the self from our modern picture by digging into components that contribute to our whole personhood. I believe there are key pillars to help a deep rediscovery. First and foremost, we absorb what God says about us in our image-bearing beauty. Then we learn to build from the stories of our ancestors and how they contribute to our identity. This also speaks to how those we hold close contribute to our formation, and lastly, how our own choices in the present continue building into our pursuit for wholeness.

## THE ANCESTORS

After a lengthy list containing the heroes of the faith, chapter twelve in the book of Hebrews begins by acknowledging those who have gone before, "since we are surrounded by such a great cloud of witnesses. . . ." Let us now include those not on the list, but who faithfully rose to overcome and defy all odds.

When I think about the question "Who are my people?," I'm engaging the layers of a continuously unfolding story about my heritage and identity. It's a story worth reclaiming because contained within are more answers that explain why I am and how I'm here. My story twists and turns right across the globe. It has taken time to pull out sometimes scant and other times stunning details, and I'm certain there are still more revelations and secrets waiting to be found.

I am an immigrant to Canada, but on my mom's side my roots go back to the turn of the twentieth century by both Chinese and Japanese immigration. Every small town in Western

Canada had a Chinese restaurant or laundromat. That was my family in Bashaw, Alberta. I'm still learning about my Chinese side and specifically about the adversity they faced with discriminatory immigration and public policies. Nonetheless, they seem to have built a way to survive and propel the younger generation to integrate and live normal lives. The claim to fame for the family was my great-uncle Sy Mah, who was in the Guinness Book of World Records for the most completed marathons until bested in the late 1990s. Curiously, I hate running.

Secretive is an apt way to describe my Japanese heritage. Our story centers around the life and times of my great-grandmother Asayo Murakami. She was the last surviving "picture bride" in Canada, living to the ripe old age of 104. There's a documentary about her life if you want to dig up the National Film Board of Canada reel online. It's called *Obachan's Garden*. (If you want to watch the film, then skip these paragraphs to avoid the spoilers.) The film was initially made to coincide with her centennial and the rebuilding of the Murakami home in Steveston, British Columbia. The home sits in a shipyard and is now a national historic site. However, filming came to an abrupt halt when Great-Grandma shared a secret she had held for over eighty years. You see, Great-Grandma had a secret family back in Japan. . . . She had two daughters and then a son who died during childbirth. The death of her son brought immense shame onto her and her husband's family. Perhaps coinciding with the Great Kanto earthquake in 1923, Great-Grandma was ostracized from the family—including her surviving children—and cast away. Her choice in the matter was to leave it all behind. She boarded a ship and came to Canada as a picture bride. Once she landed, she spent her first two years working in a cannery to pay off the man who paid her passage. She had rejected his marriage arrangement on the docks of the harbor the moment she saw him. "He was too short," she said. After paying off her debt, she remarried, and the new family moved to Steveston, where Great-Grandpa applied his trade as a boat builder. I wonder if my own penchant for woodworking is somehow locked into my hands every time I make a pass with the hand plane . . .

Like every ethnic minority population, the Japanese community in the Lower Mainland was subjected to continuous discrimination from every level of government. The problem would culminate at the height of the Second World War. After the bombing of Pearl Harbor, Japanese people in America and Canada were deemed a threat to the state. Both governments began internment programs, stripping the Japanese people of all their assets and possessions, save for two briefcases per person. Those assets were later sold for pennies to white landowners to ensure there was nothing to return to. At first everyone was shipped to internment camps. My family was lucky. They weren't separated, and eventually left the camps together. Their only choice was to head off to the Prairies, some 1,250 miles away. There they toiled as laborers on a sugar beet farm. A far cry from their life on the coast. The sad part of the story is they never went back. There was nothing left to go back to. After the war ended, and the government lifted restrictions, the family eventually settled in Southern Alberta, where most stayed for their lifetimes. Great-Grandma spent most of her remaining years in Lethbridge, and her final years in Calgary. She never accepted the full terms and conditions, never learning to speak English despite eighty years in the country. I can't imagine it was easy for her, but I consider it a form of resistance she employed.

Before my grandpa passed, I tried to talk to him about his time during and after the internment. He would have been a boy, so perhaps the memories are a bit grey. He never shared more than a sentence or two. "You could never understand" is all he could muster, offering the terse reply days after my inquiries. In 1985, the Canadian government did offer reparations. Grandpa bought a new oven with the money. So I guess there's that.

More recently I've been leaning into my West Indian heritage, tracking stories of my ancestors and when they first immigrated to Trinidad. Trinidad was a colony of Britain (it's still part of the Commonwealth). It's the southernmost island in the Caribbean and bore the similar brunt of colonization as other islands. The islands were prizes for European colonizers, and enslaved West Africans the primary labor force. But once slavery was abolished, there was an immediate labor shortage. To fill the gap, rather than adopt equitable wages, the Brits employed an immigration process that turned into state-sponsored indentured servitude. Today we would use the terms *human smuggling* and *human trafficking* to describe the movement of bodies, albeit in this case perpetrated by the government. The roots I have in Trinidad come from individuals seeking a better life in the colonies, only to be duped into indentured servitude. Although our family story contains a chapter of emancipation, it's unequivocally rooted in trauma and loss. It was a trade from poverty to poverty, and all it took was a complete displacement from the land. What does being displaced from land mean for identity? I've wondered this before. My forebears left India for Trinidad, and my dad and I left Trinidad for Canada over a hundred years later, all of which disconnected us from our indigenous lands. We must appeal to the local teachers and stories to fill the gap, but it is ultimately insufficient. If you're a settler or an immigrant, or if your ancestors were enslaved, you and your forebears have been displaced from land, and that's a gap in our picture of personhood that needs filling.

The stories of my people contribute to my identity. Their legacy shapes my path. Their legacy is worth reclaiming. It's also important to acknowledge that there are those who have been stripped from their people. Many African Americans have little knowledge of their ethnicity, lost to the horrors of enslavement. Reclamation has been robbed, or at the least made much harder to recover. Then there are other times when a legacy is worth ignoring, but it still must be claimed. Those with ancestors who were slaveholders, that's a history you have to contend with. We don't choose how we become products of ancestors or, as in my case, a story rife with trauma and loss. My people, who speak into my identity, bring a legacy of subjugation and violence. It takes a curious toll.

"The memory of trauma affects us on a genetic level," says therapist and researcher Hillary McBride.

> We call this epigenetic change. . . . Findings about epigenetic change not only help us better understand intergenerational trauma but also highlight that embodiment and trauma work are political as well as personal. For example, those in marginalized communities are more likely to experience bodily based trauma. . . . Epigenetic research helps us better understand how those in marginalized communities bear the heavier burden of intergenerational trauma, and it enables us to marvel at the intergenerational resilience that has helped people survive.[2]

Trauma is in our DNA. The trite answer to systemic wrongs is often "Just get over it, that was a long time ago," as if time will heal all wounds. It doesn't. I wish I could just get over it. I wish my grandpa hadn't been interned, impacting his life and the choices he made because of it. I wish my Indian family hadn't been tricked into servitude. But that's not reality. Active work to deal with the wounds is the salve. Yes, it may take generations of work to heal, yet despite the trauma, resiliency can win. And we become more resilient the more we heal.

Once we consider the stories of our ancestors, it tends to fill in the blanks closer to home. If you're working through a lot of historical trauma, it can be somewhat of a revelation to explain dysfunction. I remember one friend who was digging into his Métis heritage who exclaimed, "This explains the drinking, Rohadi!" I'm not here to remove any individual agency, but many of you are living in the reality where there are connections explaining dysfunction. I actually hold a bit of suspicion for people who don't have dysfunction in their family. Like what kind of glorious privilege is that? Maybe they're lying. Or maybe some folks get a taste of the kingdom here and now in their healthy homes. How you are raised, after all, contributes formatively to your identity. Your parents and immediate community speak volumes into your being, and if that relationship is dysfunctional, then there's just more opportunity for resiliency, and perhaps a need for more qualified therapy.

## TREAT YO SELF

A side story in the television show *Parks and Recreation* involves two characters who take self-care to a new level of rugged consumerism. They take lavish shopping sprees and spa retreats to treat themselves whenever a situation warrants. Unfortunately for us, self-care has little to do with material purchases. I mean, spa dates and new woodworking tools sound great, if you can afford them, but they can't fix wounds incurred by our body or personhood. The inherited trauma from our ancestors, and all the trauma incurred on our bodies throughout our lives, needs to be dealt with.

I believe everyone should see a therapist at least once a year as a regular rhythm of total health. It can be as simple as learning the difference between barriers and healthy boundaries, or it may be dealing with deep anger or hurt. Seeking a professionally licensed therapist has been instrumental in leading me through some of the hardest seasons of my life. Dealing with grief, hurt, and loss requires professional help. In a very real way therapy saved me. Trauma-informed counseling is a crucial tool to cultivate healthy identity and reflects the commitment toward wholeness. This isn't your average church therapy, either. In fact, if you ever encounter some iteration of "You don't need therapy, you just need godly informed pastoral or spiritual counsel," run in the opposite direction. Profound levels of harm and abuse are perpetrated by narrow-minded Christians who are misinformed about the necessity of licensed counseling and therapy. The Bible coupled with theological beliefs can't solve everything. Sometimes a prescription does. As more of us share our therapy experiences, it legitimizes the practices and eliminates any stigmas. So don't be afraid to tell all your friends you have a great therapist.

Of note, therapy is kind of like shopping. If you're going to "treat yo self," then you ought to ensure you're comfortable with a particular therapist. There are many different kinds of practitioners with different areas of expertise. Don't be afraid to employ a more consumer mindset (despite my repeated calls to undermine consumerism) and shop around to find the right fit and the right expertise. The advent of our pandemic world has also made video sessions more commonplace. That may be your only option especially if you're not located in a metropolitan area. My current therapist is an older white man, and despite living in a large city, I have to seek expertise outside of my city (and perhaps province) to find a therapist with experience in racialized trauma. In part because the advent of racialized minorities seeking counseling for generational and systemic traumas is relatively new, the number of therapists is low. But we need them. BIPOC folks know (or perhaps don't know) the level of trauma, and frankly anger, that needs to be processed.

Lastly, I know counseling and professional therapy is a privilege. Great expertise costs a lot of money, and it's not accessible to all. It's easy for me to write "Go see a therapist when your body is hurt" when I have medical coverage to handle the expense. Although there are sliding-scale options in many practices, it's worth putting aside some funds for professional help.

## GRIEF

The last aspect associated with paying attention to the ways our bodies absorb loss is the connection to deconstruction. Deconstruction inevitably leads to a level of grief as we process both the harm and losing past experiences and relationships. In my first church plant we tended to attract a lot of hurt Christians who never dealt with that hurt head-on. Hurt people usually spill their hurts to the community. Sometimes the community can handle it well. We didn't have the energy or expertise. Right now, in the new iteration of Cypher Church, things are very different. Once again, we have a lot of people searching to make sense of their faith, most deconstructing out of bad evangelical experiences. The difference now, however, is vulnerability. There is a humility associated with knowing you don't have any answers. There is a humbleness associated with one another's journey through past wounds. We cherish the chance to search for something better with other people longing for the same. This posture to hold space for one another has led to some profound moments of shared revelation within the community. And we've done this despite using online video and being situated in different places across the country. This profound connectedness is especially crucial right now in our age of disconnection because of the global pandemic.

There's no time frame or formula for when or how long it takes to process grief. If you have spent decades in churches, walking away is loss regardless of how necessary moving is. There is a real impact when we are torn from our past and present. But when we take our whole health seriously, we will always be at odds with the world that detracts from full belonging and ultimate freedom. Give yourself ample grace along this journey. It's not a linear progression. It's unlearning and relearning, coupled with the trauma that comes along with it. At times it may seem like you're going around in circles. But lingering in place is in fact progress, a pause to deepen roots and recalibrate your bearings. So wherever you're reading these next few chapters, put your feet to the ground and feel the heartbeat in the land.

*     *     *

To return to Brené Brown, do you belong to yourself so deeply that you share without reservation your most authentic self to the world? Knowing who you are is crucial to belonging. There are no mistakes and no software updates along the way. To know yourself is to unlock these very good distinctive features in body, mind, and spirit that form the authentic you. This person is affirmed both by God and by the people who shape you. It also means the only person who genuinely knows you is you.

Sounds obvious, but trusting yourself is often a challenge. Many of us who grew up in the church have heard the love commandments before, but few have been discipled on how to love thyself in healthy ways, if at all. It's ironic in a way, given how individualistic our society is (which includes the church). We don't have any qualms about individualizing salvation by employing a reductionist gospel of a "sinner's prayer." But many traditions struggle with formation surrounding loving thyself. We know how to deny thyself, but love? Sometimes it seems that if we're not hurting ourselves trying to fit in, we're doing the wrong things. This is the result when our perceptions of self are generated not by what God says about us, but by the characteristics of that dominant body described earlier in the book. And therein lies the problem. In the pursuit for some semblance of belonging we wind up giving up a piece of ourselves. The cultural equivalent is the work of "keeping up with the Joneses." It's a posture and activity that actually works against our pursuit for wholeness because rather than discovering and growing our own identity, we vainly try to match someone else's. This diversion effectively impedes the pathway to knowing thyself—and if we don't know ourselves, how can we love ourselves?

The solution means rejecting outside affirmations that try to dictate our fundamental identity. That will inevitably come at a cost, pushing you into the wilderness experience Brown speaks to. But there's no other way to reveal a deeper reflection of your utmost humanity and the distinct image-bearing likeness you have. It's the display of the authentic you, the authentic self, expressed in an authentic love of self.

## REFLECTIONS

Ultimately, "Who am I?" must link to Jesus and the commandment to love. We make our attempts to love in its various forms because we are first the recipients of God's love. That means the beginnings of loving thyself, and truly knowing thyself, find a suitable starting point within God's creation story. We are beloved image bearers made in the very image of the Creator. Indeed, you are a spectacle of beauty in the eyes of God, and walking toward this beauty is where our wholeness is found. It's not always *easy* (after all, love isn't easy), especially for people on the margins. But our reflection is innate. It can't be removed. We can also draw deeper to God as well. That promise to Abraham is our promise too. We are invited to be part of God's family, an ultimate form of belonging. The invitation is marked by the Holy Spirit in us, and when coupled by the symbolic rebirth in baptism, we embody new creation (2 Corinthians 5:17).

Too often the "self" is dissociated from our fundamental identity as described by God and replaced by cultural norms that demand we be something we are not. To fulfill our longing to be whole in our own bodies, we need to accept a full embodied love for who God has made us to be. From our gender and ethnicity to our sexuality and neurodiversity—all beautiful things within the image-bearing creative plan. Although such revelation may not happen all at once, like some miraculous conversion, each of us must nonetheless discover liberation tied to our mind, body, and spirit.

That's admittedly challenging for those of us who don't fit the dominant normative body. It's especially troublesome when our bodies are firmly placed outside delineated barriers to belonging erected by those we cherish and love. But there's nothing we can ever do to fit in, although some certainly try to subdue or hide their full selves for just a taste of lingering belonging. But that's not where our whole selves are found—in the shadows. I watch as queer folks walk into their liberation while simultaneously knowing who will ostracize them from community. Disabled bodies absorb the struggle to even have an opportunity to cross the outskirts of community, let alone feel the welcoming embrace.

The cost is real. And sometimes it's easier to keep your head down and hide. But how long can we survive, alone, in the wilderness? There is some consolation within the desolation. Although marginalized people may encounter community spaces denying life and belonging, we fit into the radical inclusivity and love championed by Jesus. Christ is on our side, or rather by our side, as we face the wilderness. Our authentic self remains rooted in our image-bearing goodness and cannot be undone by any manner of theological creed or doctrinal statement. That may not be helpful in particular moments (or seasons). It may sound trite to say, "Don't feel bad, God loves you!" Well if that is so, why is belonging so hard to find?

We have to hold the tension of belonging as we give ourselves more permission to find the ways we can love ourselves. As God so loves you, specifically you in your body, receive the affirmation that you are wonderfully made. This wide acceptance opens the door to walk with God into liberation and ultimate wholeness. Not only for ourselves, but a collective freedom in the context of life-giving community as well.

PART IV

# BEAUTIFUL TALES

# 10

# Newness

**IN DECEMBER 2016,** my first church plant held its last service. Together with a different team, three months later, during Valentine's week, we launched a new church called Cypher Church. If you're familiar with hip-hop culture, the cypher is a space where artists, musicians, dancers, poets, lyricists, and MCs create. Each one brings their craft to contribute, and will sometimes go toe-to-toe for bragging rights. We leveraged the experience of the cypher, inviting the community, plus onlookers who wanted to participate, and postured each creative expression in the cypher as an *offering*. Everyone was invited to bring their talent into the center and give it up to the community (or to God). Simple enough? It is if you've been in one before. If not, it's a bit intense to experience. There are no casual onlookers when the room shapes into a circle of bodies and the band fills the air with sound. Everyone participates, whether you're trying to fade into the background, or you have something to offer. Holding space for anybody, no matter their skill or voice, created incredible moments of artistic and spiritual expressions.

Our launch evening exceeded our expectations. We booked the band (they played nonstop all night), invited friends in the hip-hop and arts community, and put the call out to Christian folks who were interested in our community; the rest was in God's hands. One thing I didn't initially anticipate was how many Christians would show up just to check out the next cool church in town. I noticed them because it reminded me of a culture I had worked so hard to get away from years earlier. Most of them didn't stay past launch night, and the ones who did stay did so because they caught a glimpse of belonging they had never experienced in a church before.

So much of our Western Christianity is understood through the rigid Sunday morning service. For many, the Christian experience is defined by service components of prayer, listening or singing some songs, and then listening again to someone preach. Same rhythm fifty-two weeks a year. This isn't to dissuade the practices that work for some, but I, like many others, don't get much out of it. The challenge for people like me is that nearly every church has some iteration of the "five songs and a thirty-minute sermon" model. If you don't fit the model there are few alternative expressions within Christianity to resonate with. We lack churches with imagination for different worship expressions beyond the norm (having an evening service doesn't count). That's what Cypher Church created, and for many searching souls, it was life-giving to be *seen* in new ways.

Most worship experiences are framed within order and control. It's a posture of routine coupled with passive observance. Traditions that use a shared lectionary dictate how churches across the globe will worship on any given Sunday. It's powerful to acknowledge worldwide connection, but it's also stifling to creativity. We tried the opposite—cultivate the unexpected by inviting greater participation and creativity in worship. But there was a catch. More invitation to participate meant being vulnerable with other people. Vulnerability is a chance to be seen, but it's also a struggle to experience it. People on the margins get this. We're slow to let down our guard because we don't want to absorb unsolicited conflict or get hurt. I've been guilty of too quickly thinking I was in safe spaces only to wind up with a rude surprise. The trouble is, we can't live our true authentic selves without exposing our vulnerabilities. To find belonging, we have to put ourselves out there (again), and it may backfire. It's one of the riskiest things we can do, but we have to take the risk because we need healthy spaces to belong in order to survive (the global pandemic continues to teach us about these dimensions) and, ultimately, to thrive. Our liberation is reliant on belonging—not only to ourselves, but with others in relationship.

The search to be seen fully for who we are in loving community, to be celebrated for our gifts and abilities in our skin, is one of our innate human longings. Plus, it's always more fun to share community with friends who want to subvert anti kingdom powers and pursue justice. That's in fact the reclamation of what the church should be. As theologian Drew Hart explains, "If God is a God of justice, then worshiping communities that radically reorganize the lives to the reality of the Most High God will increasingly, and inevitably, begin participating in the revolutionary vocation of the church."[1] When you manage to taste this kind of community, it's lifegiving. I call these moments, or these seasons, beautiful tales.

I was constantly blown away by the different ways the Spirit of God would show up at our service. We had a real "early church" vibe because what I saw, and what others encountered, had no frame of reference. They were truly new experiences in worship. Invitation to connect through movement, dance, music, lyrics, and paint unlocked new ways for people to connect with God. It was overwhelming for some.

For others it was just plain fun. To move freely as worship was an exercise of liberation! That was the beauty with our approach, but it wasn't without risk. We had no control over who showed up to our events, and when you build inclusive space, inviting anyone to be seen, anything can happen.

## SHOULD YOU STAY OR SHOULD YOU GO?

It's one thing to deconstruct and leave your faith altogether. It's another to find a pathway to reclaim a more beautiful way (they are not necessarily mutually exclusive). But it's completely different practice—and dare I say essential—to *embody* the teachings of Jesus within the context of life-giving community. This is where beauty is cultivated and transpires. It sounds so good! So where can we find it and what attributes should we be looking for?

Earlier, in chapter 3, I shared four common options for belonging in church communities. In a moment I will reveal the fifth option, but first, a quick review applying some of the new awareness we've developed.

The first option in the search for belonging is to assimilate into dominant (usually white) churches. That's the most prevalent option, although as demographics shift, white dominance is changing. The second, for those who have this option, is to stay in or return to ethnic churches. That's not to imply that ethnic churches are without their own problems. Although there is an automatic benefit when you don't have to explain your ethnic presence, these traditions often inherit or assume features from the dominant culture in thought and belief. Take, for example, patriarchy. I can't think of many established ethnic traditions that don't have some legacy connection with patriarchy. On one hand an ethnic church tradition may have a clear value for dismantling white supremacy in public, but on the other hand the tradition may hold obvious prejudices in gender and sexuality. These churches are not safe spaces for all, as they don't embody radical inclusivity for all. There is a level of theological dissonance employed when racialized justice excels but gender or LGBTQIA minorities are maligned. Although it's not this simple (or perhaps it is), you can't claim one and not the other. We have to admit these traditions must contend with the "plank" in their own eye, to understand that their call for justice in one area must coincide with a call for justice everywhere. It's liberation for all. This incongruity needs to be named, along with the reality that many ethnic traditions are not safe spaces.

Then there's option 3—build diversity—when we try to join an existing institutional (white or multiethnic) church that's trying to be inclusive. That always sounds good until the critical source of marginalization—white supremacy—is brought to the forefront. To put it bluntly, plenty of affirming churches are doing great work figuring out how to be more inclusive for marginalized folks, but these churches still can't contend with their white supremacy. This doesn't stop many Christians on the margins from spending *decades* of their life trying to point the dominant institution to become a more welcoming space. Most often this work goes unfulfilled, we experience burnout, and even worse, face abuse. The cost is great, and I determined a long time ago that I can carry only so many things before my body says, No, enough.

I acknowledge that I have many BIPOC friends (usually) happily employed within institutional Christianity. They are doing the work to lead change. If this is you, I value your presence to stay. It's harder to stay within institutional Christianity and help it change. But I wonder whether material changes can ever be made. Remember, churches are cakes that have already been baked. The questions we ask about justice today are not new. It's a problem that's decades and centuries old. What makes our current iteration any different from failed attempts from the past? To compound matters, what voice do people on the margins really have? In the classic children's book *Pinocchio*, Geppetto is the maker/father character. But for those of us who are queer, trans, disabled, BIPOC, women, or neurodiverse, leadership positions are rarely for us. We can never be Geppetto. So who exactly is going to lead option 3 churches unto better?

To complicate matters, institutions by nature are not designed to accommodate change. They are designed to remain insulated and resist change. It's rare to see substantive shifts happen in real time. That's to be expected when foundations like white supremacy are questioned. Will we ever see formative change that can one day divest beyond the exclusivity of theological whiteness? Or will we continue to encounter inflexible determination by stagnant denominations willing to make their last stand ostracizing minority bodies from communion? That's what I experienced with the Vineyard. That's what we're seeing now in major evangelical denominations like the Southern Baptist Convention that are unwilling to make sweeping policy changes to protect victims—and not perpetrators—of sexual and spiritual abuse.

Institutions, if they can accommodate it, will adopt shifts incrementally over time. Currently, denominations in Canada are struggling to find a way to faithfully embody reconciliation efforts with their Indigenous neighbors. Some traditions, like the United Church and the Anglican Church of Canada, have decades of relationships-building underneath them. Others, like most evangelical ones, are starting from scratch, relying on a minute pool of Indigenous individuals to represent the whole. The urgency surrounding recent calls for church leadership toward racialized justice is another area where most fall well short. It will take years, perhaps decades, before institutions and members put their bodies on the line (Romans 12:1) as a faithful action of God's justice (Romans 1:17). We haven't even begun to consider how long it may take denominations as a whole to pivot in their understanding of inclusion of other groups, including the disabled community in its many, many forms, neurodiverse members, and nonbinary folks.

Ultimately, small shifts aren't enough to stem the tide and fix glaring wounds in the here and now. That's not to say incrementalism can't yield results. In most ways it's the only way institutions can accommodate change—slowly over the course of decades or centuries. But people on the margins don't have the time. We need expediency. We need justice now. Is it even possible? I suppose denominations could completely recalibrate their leadership and repent of their past wrongs. But past evidence over centuries would suggest it's not going to happen in the present. We need to envision a better way forward, and here lies the crux of the matter for Christians on the margins. If we have only so much energy to invest, why would we try to change something that doesn't want to move? Why not put that energy, those talents and gifts, into a *new* thing that's not built around formative traits of white supremacy and Western imperialism?

Personally, I choose life and vitality over fear and complacency. Knowing that my energy won't change the cake after it's been baked, I have opted to work outside (or maybe on the edge of inside?) institutional boundaries. The way I see it, this leaves two primary choices in the search for belonging: create something new or collaborate with something already moving. These form the two halves of option 5.

## OPTION 5: CREATE SOMETHING NEW

In the search for belonging, joining or building new community from scratch is one possibility. It's an act of liberation when ordinary people live into their unique gifts and flourish within community. An exercise in living out the fullness of our humanity, a glimpse of God's ultimate hope for us as individuals and for the world.

When you consider option 5, what's the first thing that pops into mind? Initially you might think, "I don't have much to give" or, "I don't have the time." It may be true. It takes a certain amount of resourcing to start new things. But if you're always on the search for belonging, and it's just so hard to find, the prospect of being part of the solution is alluring. I invite you to consider new questions like "How can I make a difference?" and "What gifts do I have to contribute?" We all have important attributes that make community whole. To explain, we turn to the book of Ephesians.

The general letter to churches in Ephesus offers several insights about church function that we can apply today. In chapter 4 we start with a calling.

> Conduct yourselves with all humility, gentleness, and patience. Accept each other with love, and make an effort to preserve the unity of the Spirit with the peace that ties you together. You are one body and one spirit, just as God also called you in one hope. There is one Lord, one faith, one baptism, and one God and Father of all, who is over all, through all, and in all. (Ephesians 4:2–6)

Verse 2 offers a clear explanation of what Christians are called to do: bear one another with love; be humble, meek, and patient in every way. Verse 3 kickstarts what may have been an early church creed on unity and oneness. The church is to be of "one body and one spirit; one hope; one Lord, one faith, one baptism; and one God and Father of all . . ." Unity is the central theme for Christians to embody. Ephesus was a metropolitan city, so unity as a foundational principle to Christian identity was reflected in the radical inclusivity embodied by local churches. Unity in diversity is cherished. But pay close attention to the nuance. Unity does not imply assimilation or *sameness*. Rather, this unity says bring your gifts, talents, traits, and ethnicity to share in *oneness* (one body and one spirit, one Lord and one faith, etc.). This communal posture is distinctly triune too. We reflect how the Trinity retains uniqueness in each person of Father, Son, Holy Spirit. Each keeps their unique personhood as we each keep our identity yet share in the oneness of Christ in community.

> God has given his grace to each one of us measured out by the gift that is given by Christ. (Ephesians 4:7)

Verse 7 provides insight on how a church is built. God gives each person gifts—an equipping—to build Christ's body (the church). The purpose of this work is repeated in verse 13, which, once again, is to build unity. We should emphasize how *all* are given foundational gifts that contribute to the building and function of healthy church community. There is no prerequisite for the noted Ephesians gifts of prophet, evangelist, shepherd/teacher, and apostle. They aren't reserved for a qualified few with degrees or experience. We must also highlight that there is no gender qualification either. All means all. All are commissioned to live out their gifts in their unique voice. Or to put it in another way, Christ has already given us our gifts and now we are called to flourish in them. Ironically, the idea that "everyone gets to play" is a moniker from the Vineyard church movement. The same one that concluded by committee that "everyone" really meant "everyone except if you're queer."

Ephesians offers a snapshot of early church DNA. (A similar description found in 1 Corinthians 12 is given to the church in Corinth.) What does this tangibly look like today? To answer we need to deconstruct what counts as life-giving Christian community. Starting new church community is often filtered through the gatekeeping and the vocation called church planting. We need to expand this categorization. I want to divest from the thinking that you need to be a church planter to start churches. That usually means competencies built around denominationally approved qualifications. It's certainly useful if you're putting together the prototypical church with a weekly service and small groups. But we have enough of those. Also, I'm not suggesting that licensing bodies or pastoral training is unnecessary—it is one of the gifts after all—but we ultimately don't need permission to discover our liberation.

This is coming from someone who has every denominational qualification of church planter. Originally, I jumped through the hoops to be a church planter with an evangelical denomination and passed all the assessments, but that's a different story. If you don't know anything about church planting, then good. There's nothing to unlearn. Many Christians were made to believe that only those who have special calling can create. Or that only those who have gone to seminary can lead. Or that a church must meet regularly on Sunday, and must have a certain number of people, to count as a church. But none of this is required. The point is each of us has gifts to build something different and we don't need permission to make it happen.

This may upset leaders in the contemporary church who inherit positional authority in the day-to-day lives of their parishioners. But our society is quickly doing away with inherited authority. Which is to say, the church as an institution used to have say in the lives of the average person, but today, as the fastest growing religious segment is in fact no religion at all (the sociological "nones"), that inherited voice has eroded. Now authority is based on trust developed as we share life together. We still look to leaders, voices, and ideas, but authority is relationally given. It suggests that in the bid to reimagine new ways of gathering and being the church in a modern world, we need new kinds of leaders at the helm.

You may think to yourself, "But I'm not a leader," which may be true in a traditional sense. You might get nervous about the thought of speaking in front of tens or hundreds of people. But that's not the leadership I'm referring to when it comes to building new spaces of belonging, especially for people on the margins. I'm referring to the way you can lead in your gifts. We're all good at something, so what can you bring to inspire others? Share it to the world! Plus, you're not alone in this (or hopefully you're not alone for long.) Building new is for you and your crew to do. A small group of people who are trying to embody love for God, the other, each other, and thyself, as best they can. That's kind of what Cypher Church has wound up being after nearly four years.

The gatherings at Cypher Church have never looked "normal" in reference to what constitutes a contemporary church service. However, each one has been deeply formative and life-giving. Initially, we held large events commanding a lot of musical resources. However, the cypher ran its course after about a year and a half. I was left with a decision: carry on or change how we gather. We opted for the latter.

We dwindled in number from around one hundred to a core group of around twenty. That core—some Christian, some not—began exploring ideas surrounding worship and spiritual connection. We opened the door to linger in new ways to connect and celebrate what God was doing in our midst, and to be formed in new ways to be in loving community. We adopted what artist Makoto Fujimura calls "the journey into theological thoughts through the act of making, rather than [the consumption of] rational and propositional theological information."[2] With a rough plan for each gathering built around one central idea or concept, we relied on each other to bring specific insight and expertise to the table.

Our gatherings meandered around many different artistic expressions, including evenings devoted to words. Poetry or spoken word nights were popular additions. We would start with a theme, write while jazz music plays, and return to share/listen to the ways God is moving in the community. Art nights with charcoal (seeing the image-bearing beauty in one another), paints (abstract interpretations of God in our midst), and pencils were all mediums we employed.

Perhaps the most unusual yet inspiring moment for our community was an evening devoted to "empathy through movement." Someone put together the idea and wanted to test it. The purpose: embody an exercise to *see* one another. The evening combined dance movement with intentional pauses to look and see each other in space. Literally lingering and looking into each other's eyes, touching the soul, as affirmation of both "I see you" and "I'm willing to be seen." Some things you can't fully describe, and this evening was one of them. Have you ever had a worship evening like this? One thing I can say for certain—I had never before had a moment, especially within a Christian context, that broke down the walls and truly embodied a posture of *empathy* shared together as community.

Ultimately, there is some inertia to overcome when embracing the possibilities of option 5 community. Most of us have been trained to let the pastors/leaders do the work and make community decisions. But the need for life-giving space to truly belonging is a need *now*. We need to adjust our understanding of what counts and adopt more of a posture that looks like the church mere decades after Jesus rose from the tomb. Community spaces created for and by Christians on the margins are already happening; they just don't immediately "qualify" as "official." It might look like six to twelve friends sharing a regular meal with communion around the table. To me, this sounds very official. Not only does small count in monumental ways, but it might be all that God is calling you to. Is that hard to picture? That your Christian community from here on will be six to twelve people? If it is, perhaps there's still some deconstructing that needs to happen. Both Cypher Church and the Urban Indigenous Circle, both around twenty or so core people, are in the same city, but few outsiders know either one exists.

As we dismantle the thought that size is related to legitimacy, knowing small counts in big ways helps us picture life-giving community that's within our grasp. Take a look around you. What are you already doing? Maybe you already meet for book club. Maybe you have safe space already but the topic of adding a spiritual layer hasn't come up. Lean into the possibilities. You may be surprised to see where God is already on the move.

One inevitable question as we pursue creating new is how to prevent repeating the errors from the past. How can we be sure a community will interrogate, let alone divest itself from, white supremacist theology and practices? How can we build new skills around embodied justice and wholeness? How will we know whether we're building inclusive community? As we become alert to the ways we have been shaped and formed, we hope to ask deeper questions and challenge old formation, but there's always a chance that we will replicate marginalization. That's both a relief and a constant threat. It's a relief because we don't have to be perfect to try something new with a few faithful friends. But also, we must be alert for the things we've missed along the way. More importantly, we must look for communal practices that constantly rethink whether the most marginalized are welcomed to the center.

## ANOTHER OPTION 5 POSSIBILITY: COLLABORATE

Another option 5 possibility is joining an existing church embodying a renewed way of being. There is some prework required to properly assess potential communities. The one significant difference between option 5 churches and option 3 (build diversity) is this: Option 5 churches *start* with shared values of radical inclusivity. They are the cakes baked with new ingredients. But can we check the ingredients list before joining? Usually you have to risk it and find out, putting your-self on the line once again. Another way, which is especially pertinent for those churches claiming to be multiethnic, is to do a survey of current leadership—at the denominational level, lead pastor, elders board, deacons, and so forth. The results usually reveal the power holders. You may discover a so-called multiethnic community is so in name only. Perhaps the congregation is multiethnic but the power brokers remain white men. When you do find hopeful possibilities, the next step is to figure out whether the church will practice what it preaches, starting with you. Are you fully seen in the com-munity? Is your voice and body reflected in the church, from pulpit to music to community building?

Our own formation—the "Who am I?" question—is also integral to our search for healthy church community. To know thyself means a continuous shaping of self in the present. It helps to identify weird moments and malformed ideas early on, and to avoid spaces unable to draw toward unity and inclusivity. Part of this skill is developed by what we consume. Who we read, the podcasts we listen to, the videos we watch, and so forth shapes our understanding of faith and community. Are these voices diverse? Do they have a track record of embodied practices in diverse communities? Do they challenge us to expand our idea of God and justice? Of course, all of this is a moot point if you can't find a suitable community to begin with. The options may be limited in your part of the world. Perhaps you can start searching online for some semblance of community? Today, Cypher Church does not gather in person. COVID-19 changed all of that. We are like many others—gathering online for what is now over two years. Yet meeting online has opened the door to try new things and in fact expand inclusion. It's often easier for folks with disabilities to be present and participate.

Meeting online has also enhanced collaboration. We now gather with others from different cities since video doesn't have any geographic limits. For someone who thought not ten years ago that online church was a disembodied experience and should be avoided, I repent of this position now. I mean, yes, it would be wonderful if we could all gather around the table instead of virtually, but the new online relationships found during this season are beautiful. Small and online count as legitimate church expressions. Plus, we don't need permission to invest in spaces that are devoted to the shared liberation of all people.

Our search for belonging brings us back again to the question, How do we know? How do we know when we've found a healthy and loving community? I think part of it relies on affirmation. Not from others initially, but by trusting yourself

to know in body and soul that you have found a home. I
acknowledge that some may not have good examples of
healthy home to rely on, but we can still picture the *idea* of
feeling at home. The place where we can drop our guard and
be our whole selves. The feeling of being totally seen, in full,
in community. The affirmation that your skills and abilities
count to the well-being of the whole. A space where you—and
people like you—can belong. I admit that writing about this
kind of community seems more fantasy than real. A church
that shares a pursuit of righting wrongs in your midst, and
delights in embracing new stories from the margins? It sounds
too good to be true. Do such communities even exist? And
where they do, are they not exceptionally rare? Perhaps. But
that shouldn't stop us from imperfectly reaching into community in the present and trying to glimpse this reality in the here
and now. That effort is worth it because contained within the
pursuit is a chance to be free from all that seeks to make us
less whole.

# 11

# Free

**THE THING ABOUT BELONGING?** It's just so hard to find. I knew that well before I started this book. I also knew that I was going to struggle to find a suitable ending. I tried to ignore it at first, thinking, I'll figure it out by the time I finish. My apprehension was based on the simple fact that I'm still searching for belonging. I'm still pursuing wholeness and ultimate liberation from all that seeks to make those on the margins less. In my search I have yet to arrive, and I'm not sure I know anybody who has.

It's challenging to hold this kind of uncertainty. So much of our understanding in the world is rooted in a desire for resolution. We want to start with "Once upon a time" and end with "happily ever after." Don't get me wrong, I think there *is* a happily ever after in this age and the one to come. So it's not entirely accurate to say I don't know how this is all supposed to end. I do know how it *all* ends within God's story for creation. All things will be made right. How that comes to completion is God's mystery, but we do know it's reliant on Jesus. Defeating all the powers that seek to make us, and creation, less whole inaugurates all the possibilities for ultimate liberation and freedom. Having said this, I still don't know the ending of my own story, which is suitable in a way, as it matches the fundamental question on belonging. All we have, which is quite profound, are pathways to reclaim belonging, and stories of how we reclaim pieces of our whole being along the way. Which makes stories an intrinsic offering to help others find glimpses of true belonging in their own journey. Sometimes it's all we have—our stories.

\*     \*     \*

*Kananaskis, Alberta (again).*
I'm packed and ready to go for another mountain adventure. I take the highway west from my house and reach the foot of the Rocky Mountains. After a forty-minute drive I hang a left around Morley and take Highway 40 south. I'm back in Kananaskis, and after another forty minutes, I pull over just short of Highwood Pass—Canada's highest paved road. At this elevation winter comes early. Sometimes it never leaves. Although it's the end of August, I can see skifts of snow from the night before. The forecast says sunny skies, so it should warm up as I begin another ascent. I grab my gear, add another layer of clothing, and start walking along a dry creek bed searching for the trailhead. The air is chilly enough that I can see my breath, and there's enough frost along the short mountain grass that each step leaves behind a perfect boot print.

Today's target is smaller than usual. Four hours up and down, another three thousand feet of elevation gain. The creek turns into a stream as I search for footing along the banks. The mountain walls on both sides make it hard to keep my feet dry. I finally reach a junction where three mountains meet. I see the start of the trail. This one is different in that a steep ascent happens right at the start before the trail meanders lazily to the top. Step by step by step I push through evergreens and soft moss. It's slow moving to the top.

As the trees thin, I have to stop to remove my layers. The weather app was right, it's hot today, and the heat is melting the snow and dew as forest smells of pine needles and green moss emerge from the ground. Once I hit the ridge it's a short jog (if one is inclined) to the top. I walk to the false summit (every mountain seems to have a false summit that tricks you into thinking you've reached your destination early, only to reveal another level before the eventual prize) before a short climb up more jagged rocks to the true summit.

At the top I breathe deep through the nose till my lungs are full. The hair on the back of my neck stands. At the top there's always a spiritual awakening of sorts if you let it happen. The purity of this moment pulls me deeper into the environment. Breathe in deep and full. Hold. Exhale slow. Exhale all the confusion, stress, calamities, and doubts. Life in, tribulations out.

From this height I gain new perspective about the world. I can see for a hundred miles. But it's also the problem. I have no idea what's happening below. All I see are grey mountain ranges dotted with trees. It's barren. At the top there's a distinct lack of perspective. A disconnection with the world. It's a surreal place—a thin space. Not just the air, but a space where physical and spiritual worlds collide. Maybe that can be said of any place since it's only our perception that seeks to separates these two realities.

Before I leave I want to investigate something I was eyeing during lunch. I noticed this mountain goes even higher, and since I'm here . . . I have to crawl on all fours to survey the one option: to get to the true summit I'd have to traverse a ridge about thirty feet in length and a mere eighteen inches in width. I suppose it's possible, but it's also a sheer drop to the bottom on *both* sides. I consider the prospects for an instant before admitting to myself this risk isn't worth it. It's time to go back down.

Down always takes less time but plays extra havoc on the now weary legs and knees. I take fewer breaks but the chance of making a wrong step and going for tumble increases. The midday heat is now out in full force as I take in the fullness of the mountain sun. This will only enhance my summer tan, or rather, my natural brown hue.

After carefully plodding my way back down the steep trail-head, I'm back at the creek. Only this time it's full of activity. Rock climbers have filled the banks and families are having picnics. I'm not worried about slipping into the creek, and I even dip my feet for an instant to cool them down. My wet footprints leave temporary marks on the rock shores to mark my departure. Fall is just around the corner; the deciduous trees are changing color to foretell its arrival.

## RHYTHMS TO FREEDOM

On the mountain that day I experienced a microcycle of all four seasons. An apt metaphor for the journey of deconstruction. As we engage with the barriers to belonging, we are bound to face all the emotions attributed with the seasons. Death and change associated with the fall. Grief and desolation with winter (think especially of a frigid Canadian winter). The possibilities of reclamation birthed in the spring. Moments where we teeter on the proverbial edge of just leaving it all behind. Then comes summer, when a new rhythm of life takes hold.

Despite the rhythm of new seasons, obstacles never seem to fail to emerge, like those barriers inhibiting belonging. This tension, coupled with the current inequity in our world, constantly reminds us that things are not the way they should be. How our world works, and how the church operates too, is built around barriers that prevent us from being whole. So we search for better, doing the work to name all the evil systems and powers we must divest from in order to be free. This process leads us into deconstruction, into the process of discarding, keeping, and reclaiming new ways of being free. Nonetheless, it's tiresome to face constant impediments, to the point that walking away from faith or the church looks good.

But when we linger we resist.

We resist with a specific type of resistance: joy. Through all the forces that seek to make us less whole, *joy* from the margins becomes resistance to all that ain't right in the world. But is it enough? Resistance is exhausting. Sometimes we just want to unplug. Plus, is it up to us to confront the powers on our own?

As we absorb all the features seeking to make us less whole, the constant pursuit of belonging, the unending cycle of grief from deconstruction, the injustice that's committed against our bodies and those we love, the work we must do to control trauma from the past, all of this weight—the marginalization, the racism, the sin, our own sin, our yearning for true belonging—amounts to this: *God wants you to be free from this pain.* Free from loss, grief, despair, hurt, anger, loneliness, injustice . . . Free. A freedom we can touch and claim because the Son has set us free (John 8:36).

Exhale.

Jesus shares a story specifically for those of us caught in this struggle. An offer of respite. In Matthew 11:28–30 he says, "Come to me, all you who are struggling hard and carrying heavy loads, and I will give you rest. Put on my yoke, and learn from me. I'm gentle and humble. And you will find rest for yourselves." Every motion we take to embody the character of Jesus is a move unto life, rest, and freedom. There's solace here. To be free. Not the freedom to do as we please and fill every individual desire. But a freedom to walk in a renewed way in this world. Freedom to be as we were made to be—in full—and to be with others. This requires a reorientation, a spring renewal of thinking, believing, but most of all a reclamation of our identity in Christ. These reclaimed pieces of love, justice, beauty, and a story of future hope are worth keeping. There are stories from our ancestors worth learning from. It's work to rediscover a healthier you, all while appealing to new sources contributing to a hopeful story about belonging.

## TRUE BELONGING

We all want to belong. To have purpose—to matter in our own story, which is very much a shared human story. When we find healthy ways to fill these longings, we capture more beauty in our humanity. As belonging goes, it's not how well you belong to yourself, although that's crucial too, but rather how we belong to one another and the other. How we belong to the land and to God. How we belong with the things that God intrinsically values. Belonging starts here, but it must also extend. Belonging is found in the reclamation of a faith that begins on the margins. We are *reclaiming Christianity on the margins*. Not to bring the margins to a new center, but to meet Jesus there—on the margins. In Jesus we discover the source to right relationships, first with God, and then with others (Acts 13:38–39). In the style of last shall be first, and first last, on the margins I have more in common with Jesus than I would at the top of the mountain.

The upturning of all things that ain't right in the world is dealt with by Jesus, who inaugurates a new world with new possibilities. Because we have the resurrection, God's unfolding hope for the renewal of all things—to ultimately turn all the wrongs right—is happening now. Power has been stripped from all the anti-kingdom systems by Jesus, who now first invites the margins to embody a new way of being built around radical inclusive love. Love is the ethic for those who want to be truly free. It draws us to choose a distinct posture within the tensions of the "now but not yet." As a more beautiful way was inaugurated at the cross and then the tomb, we carry on a new hope for the ultimate restoration of broken things in our world. We believe this plan unfolds here on the earth. The Christian faith does not rest in the escape to heaven in the clouds; rather, it holds an embodied hope in reclamation of all things here and now. It's heaven *here*, on earth. All the wrongs, the injustice, the pain and trauma, rescued and restored *now* in our time. But it's not yet. We face the burden of imposing powers that undermine love and liberation. That's why it's so important to take on the vocation of love and all it entails, like justice, beauty, and ultimate belonging.

And what about liberation unto ultimate wholeness? True belonging is embodied with the expansive connection employed in a posture of abundant love. Abundance works against our common systems in our world. Our economies are rooted on the base understanding of fundamental scarcity. But love is in abundance because it's Christ who freely gives. That doesn't mean it doesn't *feel scarce* at times. Despite a lifetime of trying to fit in, and seeing how we are marginalized, I still hold my faith for this reason—abundant love.

## LIBERATION, FLOURISHING, AND TRUE BELONGING

What does it look like to not merely survive but flourish? When you have, or find, your people, the difference is feeling that you can exhale and just be yourself. To be seen in your own skin. Letting your hair down gives life. That doesn't make community, and the relationships inside, easy. The reality for Cypher Church, as an affirming church with roots toward inclusivity, is that we live these things imperfectly. We want to love in all ways but fail often. Embodying the character of Jesus and his teachings with other people is hard. This is why we rely on so much grace. We need it, especially in times when conflict arises. That happened to us when we faced choices surrounding race and LGBTQIA inclusion. It's happening now given our pro-vaccine and high health precaution stance. Loving one another is hard, and Jesus takes us one step more. Not only are we called to love one another, but we are called to love our enemies too. We don't even know how to have an enemy,[1] let alone love them. That's on top of loving ourselves and digging deep into the aspects that can make us whole.

But that's where life-giving community should step up. It's easier to opt for disembodied practices like reading a book, scrolling through social media for daily quips, doing self-care, or visiting special events that only scratch the surface of deeper questions about belonging. It's harder—but this is where the substantive elements of belonging are found—to venture imperfectly in a community embodying practices of holistic love for all. When we are seen—and work to ensure that others are seen as well—we join an environment where each relational connection between people, land, and God flourishes.

Our story won't end as we find these life-giving spaces. After all, although some of the pursuit for belonging is individual, the implications stretch beyond. When we practice a more beautiful way, we demonstrate new possibilities for the future. We join in the creation of beauty through the repair of broken things that may transpire over the course of *generations*. It's belonging and liberation for me *and* for those who are coming and will no longer have to contend with being overlooked. Now that sounds like justice.

We end with a final story. In the gospel of Luke (Luke 14:7–24), Jesus is around a dinner table (yet again) and notices how the guests are vying for choice seating. Jesus intervenes with a cheeky parable, saying those who lift themselves up will be brought low, and those who make themselves low will be lifted up. Another version of last shall be first and first last. Someone in the back is just happy to be in the room and adds, "Blessed are those who will feast in God's kingdom!" Jesus then replies with a description of what that table will look like.

> A certain man hosted a large dinner and invited many people. When it was time for the dinner to begin, he sent his servant to tell the invited guests, "Come! The dinner is now ready." One by one, they all began to make excuses. The first one told him, "I bought a farm and must go and see it. Please excuse me." Another said, "I bought five teams of oxen, and I'm going to check on them. Please excuse me." Another said, "I just got married, so I can't come." When he returned, the servant reported these excuses to his master. The master of the house became angry and said to his servant, "Go quickly to the city's streets, the busy ones and the side streets, and bring the poor, crippled, blind, and lame." The servant said, "Master, your instructions have been followed and there is still room." The master said to the servant, "Go to the highways and back alleys and urge people to come in so that my house will be filled. I tell you, not one of those who were invited will taste my dinner." (Luke 14:15–24)

This parable is often mistaken as an example for poor wedding etiquette. The invited guests make insulting excuses for why they can't attend despite advanced notice. Then the host, in a fit of "I'll show them," opens the banquet to anybody he can find on the street. The house servant replies, "That's been done, but there's still room." Did you catch it? The wedding guests who made up excuses and declined the invitation *chose not to attend*. It's not that they couldn't go, but rather that they *wouldn't*. Why? Because of the notoriety of the host. He is known for inviting certain kinds of guests to his feasts. The poor, the crippled, the blind, and the lame. The guests who thought highly about themselves opted to dissociate from a host who sent the first invitations to people on the margins of society! If we pay attention to the short note in Sarah Ruden's translation we discover the host expands the invitation even further. He tells the house servant to go into the country and invite not only the urban beggars, but the even poorer country laborers. If we want a picture of God's radical inclusion, this parable reveals who is invited to feast at God's table. All are welcome, with specific inclusion to the wide margins.

## THE FINAL TABLE

Do you remember the three vignettes of belonging at the start of chapter 2? Let's go back to the dinner table to close our journey. It's the same table, but this time it's about who is present.

Alyssa and I are hosting, getting the meal ready.

Over in the corner, there's Maria. She never comes to our services but will happily talk about spiritual things at the dinner table.

Amanda is here too; she recently separated from her husband.

Ophelia is their usual self. They're queer and happily engage conversation about their sexuality, although they haven't come out to their parents yet.

Suzi is a single mom, and she brings wee Olivia.

Spencer is here. He grew up in an evangelical church, showed up on the opening night for Cypher Church, and never left.

Riley and Robin are one of the few married couples in our midst. Neither grew up in the church but they always have something deeply spiritual to share.

Cory came late but he drove in from Morley, so we're happy he could make it.

The recovery crowd with Ty and Neil are in the corner. Neither identify as Christian, but they will pull our conversations into vulnerable spaces many Christians have trouble broaching.

And lastly, Tori is quietly absorbing it all. I'm not entirely sure what her story is, since she's new, but props to her for hanging out with a bunch of strangers.

The table invites friends new and old to share intimate connection and love without reservation. Together we hold this space of belonging, even if it's imperfect at times.

A more beautiful way takes unique shape when you and your crew deepen your identity in Christ, chase liberation, and start living out the fullness of your gifts. Within, belonging is found, joined to God's unfolding hope to rescue and redeem neighborhoods, cities, and beyond. No doubt, it's easier to walk away from the hurt and skepticism. But what it means to be truly free ironically doesn't mean walking alone. Rather, freedom is tied to belonging and liberation. When we can belong in community knowing we are fully seen in our own skin and celebrated, we begin to unlock the fullness of our image-bearing humanity. We start to experience healing, wholeness, and ultimate shalom. We live out a piece of heaven now rooted in place as we aim to embody the character of Jesus in our love for God, ourselves, those in community, and our neighbor as well. It's the response *yes* to the invitation to join God's unfolding dream in our midst. One that begins on the margins, the place where Jesus is, inviting us to the table to experience a new love that knows no bounds.

Come, dear reader, and reclaim this invitation to love and be loved. Receive now the commission to discover your liberation and experience the fullness of your humanity. May you experience profound belonging that ultimately returns you back to the Creator. May you capture a joy that knows no bounds, and a love that extends to a place where no one else will go, and then takes one step more.

# Acknowledgments

**IT IS A GIFT TO WRITE** and an even greater gift to have others absorb a written offering in a bid to discover wholeness. Thank you for taking the time to engage this body of work. If it struck a resonant chord, can I ask you for a favor? Please share it with someone who needs it. Also, don't hesitate to find me online. I love hearing stories from others who are discovering their liberation.

Writing is a lonely exercise, and writing during a global pandemic doubly so. That makes the need for a team so important. Thank you to the squad at Herald Press for seeing the value in *When We Belong*. Thank you in particular to the editors, including Laura Leonard, Sara Versluis, and Elisabeth Ivey.

Thank you, Kaitlin, for your storytelling, and for sharing your words in the foreword.

To every voice that offered an endorsement, including Terence Lester, Sarah Bessey, Gricel Medina, Gena Ruocco Thomas, Trey Ferguson, Blake Chastain, Angie Hong, Carlos A. Rodríguez, Charlotte Donlon, and Ray Aldred. Each took precious time to review this manuscript and offer words of encouragement. Thank you, Drew Hart, for making the connection. Also, thanks to Bernadette Arthur, Chad Lucas, and Monetta Bailey, who gave input on a really early version of this book.

To the ancestors who went before me and paved the way. The Nagassars, Mahs, Wongs, and Murakamis. Look at how far we've come.

Lastly, to my partner Alyssa. You gave me the space and time to spend too many evenings creating this book. Thank you for your love.

# Notes

**CHAPTER 1**

1. Find Lis Lam at TheSubversiveTable.com.
2. Mika Edmondson (@mika_edmondson), Twitter post, December 20, 2021, 8:01 a.m., https://twitter.com/mika_edmondson/status/1472945170479992834, emphasis my own.

**CHAPTER 2**

1. Charlotte Donlon, *The Great Belonging: How Loneliness Leads Us to Each Other* (Minneapolis: Broadleaf, 2020), ch. 1.
2. Maya Angelou, interview by Bill Moyers, *Bill Moyers Journal*, November 21, 1973. Transcript available at https://billmoyers.com/content/conversation-maya-angelou/.
3. Brené Brown, *Braving the Wilderness: The Quest for True Belonging and the Courage to Stand Alone* (New York: Random House, 2017), 40.
4. Sebene Selassie, *You Belong: A Call for Connection* (New York: HarperOne, 2020), 7.
5. Selassie, *You Belong*, 13.
6. John McKnight and Peter Block, *The Abundant Community: Awakening the Power of Families and Neighborhoods* (San Francisco: Berret-Koehler, 2010), 2.
7. Jacques Ellul, *If You Are the Son of God: The Suffering and Temptations of Jesus*, tr. Anne-Marie Andreasson Hogg (Eugene, OR: Wipf and Stock, 2014), 67.
8. Chief John Snow, *These Mountains Are Our Sacred Places: The Story of the Stoney Indians* (Toronto: Samuel-Stevens, 1977), 24.

## CHAPTER 3

1. Martin Luther King Jr., interview by Frank Van Der Linden, May Craig, Anthony Lewis, and Lawrence E. Spivak, *Meet the Press*, April 17, 1960. Transcript available from the Stanford Martin Luther King, Jr. Research and Education Institute at http://okra.stanford.edu/transcription/ document_images/Vol05Scans/17Apr1960_InterviewonMeetthePress.pdf.
2. Although there is some additional nuance to this claim as cities become more diverse, segregation is still prevalent. Consult the work of Michael O. Emerson, *Divided by Faith: Evangelical Religion and the Problem of Race in America* (New York: Oxford University Press, 2000) and *People of the Dream: Multiracial Congregations in the United States* (Princeton, NJ: Princeton University Press, 2006). Also see the work of Korrie Edwards.
3. The "threat versus pet" language is from Soong-Chan Rah.
4. A million is only a slight exaggeration.
5. Jemar Tisby, *The Color of Compromise: The Truth about the American Church's Complicity in Racism* (Grand Rapids, MI: Zondervan, 2018), 54–55.

## CHAPTER 4

1. W. E. B. Du Bois, *The Souls of Black Folk* (Mineola, NY: Dover, 1994). First published 1903.
2. Eric Mason, *Woke Church: An Urgent Call for Christians in America to Confront Racism and Injustice* (Chicago: Moody, 2018), ch. 1.
3. I'm not saying age is an attribute to orthodoxy, but it speaks to history beyond a Western gaze.
4. Read more about my work, including data sets on church growth, in my book *Thrive: Ideas to Lead the Church in Post-Christendom* (Calgary: RoBarry Publications, 2018).
5. "Missional church" is a missiological term used to describe the church joining God's already unfolding mission to rescue and redeem humanity as a central purpose and function, rather than an offshoot "outreach" or "program."
6. Bradly Mason (@alsoacarpenter), Twitter post, October 16, 2021, 11:07 a.m., https://twitter.com/AlsoACarpenter/status/1449421756523941891.
7. Nagassar, *Thrive*, ch. 4.
8. I use the past-tense term *was* here because we're at the precipice of a demographic shift where white evangelicals are no longer a majority segment.
9. For another definition of deconstruction, see Crystal Cheatham and Theresa Ta, eds., *The Deconstructionists Playbook: An Anthology* (Philadelphia: Bemba, 2021).

## CHAPTER 5

1. Similar work is now being done in the United States with equally shocking results.

2. See "Reports," National Centre for Truth and Reconciliation, accessed October 20, 2021, https://nctr.ca/records/reports/.

3. Truth and Reconciliation Commission, *Canada's Residential Schools: The Final Report of the Truth and Reconciliation Commission of Canada* (Montreal: McGill-Queen's University Press, 2015), 1.

4. This is a term used throughout the Truth and Reconciliation Commission report *What We Have Learned: Principles of Truth and Reconciliation* (Ottawa: Truth and Reconciliation Commission of Canada, 2015).

5. Isabel Wilkerson, *Caste: The Origins of Our Discontents* (New York: Random House, 2020), 17.

6. A definition of racism from Crossroads Anti-Racism Organizing and Training. Visit them at CrossroadsAntiracism.org.

7. Jacques Ellul, *If You Are the Son of God: The Suffering and Temptations of Jesus*, tr. Anne-Marie Andreasson Hogg (Eugene, OR: Wipf and Stock, 2014), 71.

8. Walter Wink, *Naming the Powers: The Language of Power in the New Testament* (Philadelphia: Fortress Press, 1984), 100.

9. Wink, *Naming the Powers*, 106.

10. Patricia Hill Collins and Sirma Bilge, *Intersectionality*, 1st ed. (Cambridge, UK: Polity, 2016), 7. Cited in Chanequa Walker-Barnes, *I Bring the Voices of My People: A Womanist Vision for Racial Reconciliation* (Grand Rapids, MI: Eerdmans, 2019), 64.

11. Martin Luther King Jr., "Where Do We Go from Here?" (presidential address, annual SCLC Convention, Atlanta, August 16, 1967), https://kinginstitute.stanford.edu/where-do-we-go-here.

12. Why nearly 80 percent of white evangelicals remained steadfast Republican supporters is rooted in the fear of losing inherited white cultural privileges. See Kristin Kobes Du Mez, *Jesus and John Wayne: How White Evangelicals Corrupted a Faith and Fractured a Nation* (New York: Liveright Publishing, 2021) for the full analysis.

13. Jemar Tisby, *The Color of Compromise: The Truth about the American Church's Complicity in Racism* (Grand Rapids, MI: Zondervan, 2018), 17.

14. Walker-Barnes, *I Bring the Voices*, 71.

15. The theological term for this is *telos*.

16. Sarah Augustine, *The Land Is Not Empty: Following Jesus in Dismantling the Doctrine of Discovery* (Harrisonburg, VA: Herald Press, 2021), 26.

17. Augustine, *The Land Is Not Empty*, 26.

18. Mark Charles and Soong-Chan Rah, *Unsettling Truths: The Ongoing Dehumanizing Legacy of the Doctrine of Discovery* (Downers Grove, IL:

InterVarsity Press, 2020), 15. A translation of the papal bull from Latin is available at https://doctrineofdiscovery.org/dum-diversas/.

19. Augustine, *Land Is Not Empty*, 27.

20. Willie James Jennings, *The Christian Imagination: Theology and the Origins of Race* (New Haven: Yale University Press, 2010), 59.

21. Wilkerson, *Caste*, 141.

22. Special Field Orders, No. 15, proclaimed by Union general William Tecumseh Sherman, which garnered support from Abraham Lincoln but was quickly overturned by his successor, Andrew Johnson. The idea initially came from a collective of pastors led by Rev. Garrison Frazier.

23. The term *Manifest Destiny* was first coined by John L. O'Sullivan in the *United States Magazine and Democratic Review* in 1845.

24. During this time there were also nonviolent movements working against colonial powers—Gandhi in India, Mandela in South Africa, producing eventual responses in other regions like South America. It makes you note the connection points in the present, from the Arab Spring to Occupy to Black Lives Matter.

25. *R. v. Sparrow*, [1990] 1 S.C.R. 1075. Full decision available at https://www.canlii.org/en/ca/scc/doc/1990/1990canlii104/1990canlii104.html.

26. A short and important resource to read is Bob Joseph, *21 Things You May Not Know about the Indian Act: Helping Canadians Make Reconciliation with Indigenous Peoples a Reality* (Port Coquitlam, BC: Indigenous Relations Press, 2018).

27. *Report 3—Access to Safe Drinking Water in First Nations Communities—Indigenous Services Canada* (Ottawa: Office of the Auditor General of Canada, 2021), https://www.oag-bvg.gc.ca/internet/English/parl_oag_202102_03_e_43749.html.

28. Consult Dominique Dubois Gilliard, *Rethinking Incarceration: Advocating for Justice That Restores* (Downers Grove, IL: IVP Books, 2018).

29. Read Bryan Stevenson's *Just Mercy* (New York: Spiegel and Grau, 2014) for a snapshot of the most egregious examples.

30. Willie James Jennings, *After Whiteness: An Education in Belonging (Theological Education between the Times)* (Grand Rapids, MI: Eerdmans, 2020), 15.

31. Robert P. Jones, *White Too Long: The Legacy of White Supremacy in American Christianity* (New York: Simon and Schuster, 2020), 19.

32. Recommended readings by Vine Deloria Jr. include *Red Earth, White Lies* (New York: Scribner, 1995) and *God Is Red* (Wheat Ridge, CO: Fulcrum Publishing, 2003; first published 1973).

33. Jennings, *After Whiteness*, 15.

## CHAPTER 6

1. Willie James Jennings, *The Christian Imagination: Theology and the Origins of Race* (New Haven: Yale University Press, 2010), 4.

2. Jennings, *Christian Imagination*, 6.

3. Walter Wink, *Engaging the Powers: Discernment and Resistance in a World of Domination* (Minneapolis: Fortress Press, 1992), 51–55.

4. One narrative summary about the emergence of the religious right, and how it squarely targeted marginalized groups, can be found in Deborah Jian Lee's *Rescuing Jesus: How People of Color, Women, and Queer Christians Are Reclaiming Evangelicalism* (Boston: Beacon Press, 2015).

5. Robert P. Jones, *White Too Long: The Legacy of White Supremacy in American Christianity* (New York: Simon and Schuster, 2020), 68.

6. The cake metaphor is from my friend Bernadette Arthur. Find her at ASharedTable.ca.

7. Joseph Drexler-Dreis, *Decolonial Love: Salvation in Colonial Modernity* (New York: Fordham University Press), 2–3

8. Kristin Kobes Du Mez, *Jesus and John Wayne: How White Evangelicals Corrupted a Faith and Fractured a Nation* (New York: Liveright Publishing, 2021), 141.

## CHAPTER 7

1. Lisa Sharon Harper, *The Very Good Gospel: How Everything Wrong Can Be Made Right* (Colorado Springs, CO: Waterbrook and Multnomah, 2016), 31.

2. Palmer Becker, *Anabaptist Essentials: Ten Signs of a Unique Christian Faith* (Harrisonburg, VA: Herald Press, 2017), 46–51.

3. I prefer the traditional English translation of *blessed*, but the CEB translates *blessed* as *happy*, which certainly gives a different meaning to the text.

4. These verses taken from Matthew 5 are a combination of my own translations, the CEB, and for the last verse, Sarah Ruden's translation, *The Gospels: A New Translation* (New York: Modern Library, 2021).

5. J. Denny Weaver, *The Nonviolent Atonement* (Grand Rapids, MI: Eerdmans, 2001), 79.

6. Weaver, *Nonviolent Atonement*, 45.

7. N. T. Wright, *The Day the Revolution Began: Reconsidering the Meaning of Jesus's Crucifixion* (San Francisco: Harper One, 2016), 156–57.

8. Wright, *Day the Revolution Began*, 408.

9. Weaver, *Nonviolent Atonement*, 54.

## CHAPTER 8

1. Willie James Jennings, *The Christian Imagination: Theology and the Origins of Race* (New Haven: Yale University Press, 2010), 267.

2. It's important to acknowledge the intersection of race and sexuality here. Queer BIPOC folks still encounter racism in progressive churches that are affirming.

3. Karen Keen, *Scripture, Ethics, and Same-Sex Relationships* (Grand Rapids, MI: Eerdmans, 2018), 102.

4. Theological approaches include "bounded set," a thinking that builds barriers you can't cross. Right thinking is on the right side of the fence. "Centered set" puts Jesus in the center and then dynamically moves to meet him.

5. Kristin Kobes Du Mez, *Jesus and John Wayne: How White Evangelicals Corrupted a Faith and Fractured a Nation* (New York: Liveright Publishing, 2021), 108–9.

6. Someone might be thinking of 2 Timothy 3:16 as evidence of God's hand in the Bible. I'm not saying the Spirit of God doesn't have a hand in creating the collection of titles we have today, but 2 Timothy doesn't directly refer to the Bible. When this verse was penned, canon wasn't affirmed and some letters in the New Testament were yet to be written. The original word used in 2 Timothy isn't even "scripture"—it's "writings." So perhaps this refers to pieces of parchment from the Old Testament, or a letter from an apostle . . . but not the entire Bible as we know it.

7. Beth Allison Barr, *The Making of Biblical Womanhood: How the Subjugation of Women Became Gospel Truth* (Grand Rapids, MI: Brazos Press, 2021), 149.

8. Esau D. McCauley, *Reading while Black: African American Biblical Interpretation as an Exercise in Hope* (Downers Grove, IL: InterVarsity Press, 2020), 21.

9. I've interviewed Tony on three separate episodes on my podcast, *Faith in a Fresh Vibe*. He shares some of the Stoney history, particularly the parts that encountered the first missionaries to their land. How that first relationship worked surprised me. Have a listen for the whole story.

10. "Brown Church" is a term used throughout Robert Chao Romero's book *Brown Church: Five Centuries of Latina/o Social Justice* (Downers Grove, IL: InterVarsity, 2020).

## CHAPTER 9

1. Hillary L. McBride, *The Wisdom of Your Body: Finding Healing, Wholeness, and Connection through Embodied Living* (Ada, MI: Baker, 2021), 26.

2. McBride, *Wisdom*, 91–92.

## CHAPTER 10

1. Drew G. I. Hart, *Who Will Be a Witness? Igniting Activism for God's Justice, Love, and Deliverance* (Harrisonburg, VA: Herald Press, 2020), 220.
2. Makoto Fujimura, *Art and Faith: A Theology of Making* (New Haven: Yale University Press), 89.

## CHAPTER 11

1. See Melissa Florer-Bixler's book *How to Have an Enemy: Righteous Anger and the Work of Peace* (Harrisonburg, VA: Herald Press, 2021).

# Selected Bibliography

Augustine, Sarah. *The Land Is Not Empty: Following Jesus in Dismantling the Doctrine of Discovery*. Harrisonburg, VA: Herald Press, 2021.

Barr, Beth Allison. *The Making of Biblical Womanhood: How the Subjugation of Women Became Gospel Truth*. Grand Rapids, MI: Brazos Press, 2021.

Becker, Palmer. *Anabaptist Essentials: Ten Signs of a Unique Christian Faith*. Harrisonburg, VA: Herald Press, 2017.

Brown, Brené. *Braving the Wilderness: The Quest for True Belonging and the Courage to Stand Alone*. New York: Random House, 2017.

Charles, Mark, and Soong-Chan Rah. *Unsettling Truths: The Ongoing Dehumanizing Legacy of the Doctrine of Discovery*. Downers Grove, IL: InterVarsity Press, 2020.

Cone, James H. *The Cross and the Lynching Tree*. Maryknoll, NY: Orbis Books, 2013.

————. *God of the Oppressed*. Maryknoll, NY: Orbis Books, 2019. First published 1975.

Crane, Chandra. *Mixed Blessing: Embracing the Fullness of Your Multiethnic Identity*. Downers Grove, IL: InterVarsity Press, 2020.

Curtice, Kaitlin B. *Native: Identity, Belonging, and Rediscovering God*. Grand Rapids, MI: Brazos Press, 2020.

Deloria, Vine Jr. *God Is Red: A Native View of Religion*. Wheat Ridge, CO: Fulcrum Publishing, 2003. First published 1973.

Du Mez, Kristin Kobes. *Jesus and John Wayne: How White Evangelicals Corrupted a Faith and Fractured a Nation*. New York: Liveright Publishing, 2021.

Ellul, Jacques. *If You Are the Son of God: The Suffering and Temptations of Jesus*. Translated by Anne-Marie Andreasson Hogg. Eugene, OR: Wipf and Stock, 2014.

Jennings, Willie James. *After Whiteness: An Education in Belonging (Theological Education between the Times)*. Grand Rapids, MI: Eerdmans, 2020.

————. *The Christian Imagination: Theology and the Origins of Race*. New Haven: Yale University Press, 2010.

McCauley, Esau D. *Reading while Black: African American Biblical Interpretation as an Exercise in Hope*. Downers Grove, IL: InterVarsity Press, 2020.

Nagassar, Rohadi. *Thrive: Ideas to Lead the Church in Post-Christendom*. Calgary: RoBarry Publications, 2018.

Selassie, Sebene. *You Belong: A Call for Connection*. New York: HarperOne, 2020.

Shin, Sarah. *Beyond Colorblind: Redeeming Our Ethnic Journey*. Downers Grove, IL: InterVarsity Press, 2017.

Tisby, Jemar. *The Color of Compromise: The Truth about the American Church's Complicity in Racism*. Grand Rapids, MI: Zondervan, 2018.

Weaver, J. Denny. *The Nonviolent Atonement*. Grand Rapids, MI: Eerdmans, 2001.

Wilkerson, Isabel. *Caste: The Origins of Our Discontents*. New York: Random House, 2020.

Wink, Walter. *Engaging the Powers: Discernment and Resistance in a World of Domination*. Minneapolis: Fortress Press, 1992.

———. *Naming the Powers: The Language of Power in the New Testament*. Philadelphia: Fortress Press, 1984.

Wright, N. T. (Nicholas Thomas). *The Day the Revolution Began: Reconsidering the Meaning of Jesus's Crucifixion*. San Francisco: Harper One, 2016.

# The Author

**ROHADI NAGASSAR** is a writer, entrepreneur, nonprofit developer, and pastor. He lives on Treaty 7 land in Calgary, Alberta. He currently writes in the areas of antiracist discipleship, deconstruction, and decolonizing the church. He has previously contributed in the areas of church planting, missional thinking, and  church revitalization. He is both a practitioner and a thought leader, and co-created two churches, including an inner-city multiethnic expression called Cypher Church. You can find his articles on mission and decolonizing the church at *Sojourners*, V3, New Leaf Network, Mosaic Ministries, and more. His previous books include *Soul Coats: Bible Themed Adult Coloring, Thrive: Ideas to Lead the Church in Post-Christendom,* and *#changethestory: A Short Resource on Dismantling Racism in the Church*. Visit him at Rohadi.com for more, including his podcast, *Faith in a Fresh Vibe*.